The Anatomy of Service (& Sales)

Spines

The Anatomy of Service (& Sales)

Joseph Devine

Contents

Chapter 1

Why We Serve (& sell) In Everything We Do

One of the first things we do as a newborn baby is look for someone to serve us. At this infancy stage, it's an undeveloped mind, with thousands or more years of history packed inside our newly formed "neck-top," but the bottom line is, *'We Need To Be Served'* (sooner than later, please.)

So here's this baby, brand new to the stage. Then, all of a sudden, this mother figure comes into the scene within minutes, and voila, she is serving us (in most cases, some of us do have experience with the problematic latch-on but will save it for another story.)

Service, therefore, is critical to the survival of the human race (and likely all plants and animals, and even the world.) Wait, what? Service will save the world? And is it like breastfeeding?

Yep.

Well, technically, I'm saying we like our existence and have a pretty good thing going for the most part. So maybe things are a touch more complicated than this, but follow me as I digress over the coming chapters. In the end, we will have some fun together and maybe even learn some things about how these little connections are the key to a service-mindset sales strategy...

And Yes, the difficulty with our human condition situation is and always has been a scarcity of resources. So, as time has plodded on, we humans have become better at organizing systems to ensure that everyone and everything has a fighting chance for survival. I initially wondered how I could attack such a vast subject. It's basically a cliff notes version of micro and macroeconomics (only one of which college classes I have completed.) Then, I decided this book may end up needing to be several books because the subject matter of service extends across species, nations, religions, institutions, economies, generations, and genres. Hopefully, this is a cross-generational overview book that helps us to drill down on a mindset that, once learned, will take us all wherever we want to go.

Maybe the kids could get this for graduation so they can see where to take their lives. Even if only for a roadmap on how to approach life. It's worth letting some of this stuff sink in. Read and re-read and share it with others. We can do this thing! I'm not touting becoming a salesman, which always ends in death... I'm just saying.

I didn't come up with any of these concepts on my own. These ideas and concepts are already part of the world we know. They have been for quite some time (no specifics here, just worth saying, this is ancient stuff, so we need to keep on track).

The hope is that each generation can be a bit wiser than the last, and in the end, world peace will happen. Again, I digress (yet hope does make things possible)... Maybe it is that simple.

I am, however, aware of the world around me, and through observation, trial, many errors, successes, adversity and simply by being on the front lines of sales and service since I was three years old, I have thus decided it would be wise to pass on some of my findings, to offer another perspective on what it means to serve (another run-on... oh well) other humans, animals, plants, and the world. My current gig is in the world of Green Energy, which is why I include all the animals, plants, and the world—many examples of how this sector of the economy encompasses the whole of this book follow.

There are several mindsets available for sales, but this one, 'the service mindset,' feels and works well for those who are wired this way. People are all wired a bit differently, and studying different styles is wise. Like how a doctor would employ the scientific approach to diagnosing a health case, we in sales are free to use a similar process to our trade. However, our bedside manner is what the patients remember. One must study many disciplines, like anatomy, psychology, physiology and others, to be a doctor. These chapters may strike a chord with you and will lead to growth. They will undoubtedly lead me to growth just by organizing my thoughts on this subject.

The mere fact that you are curious about how to be better at what you do, whether sales, hospitality, farming, manufacturing, or even presiding over the free world, means your curiosity puts you auto-matically toward the top of the heap. Although some presidents (the position is a service and a sales job) are more curious than others and thus are perceived by voters (your clients will be voting, by the way...) through various lenses, you get the idea. Trust is the most critical lens. But please don't bring up politics; be an excellent listener to this subject. Often, being a good poker player (political cards close to the vest) is akin to an excellent initial discussion, which then leads to better discussions, which then leads to trust, and finally an open door to service (& sales) and maybe even a bit of political banter with a friend at some point down the road.

Conversational awareness is pivotal to sales. Watch closely, learn, and choose what styles you identify with before pursuing a career in sales, for example. I like it when people are friendly to me, and they don't take advantage of me, and they care more about me than selling something. I like it when they look me in the eye and don't have any of that canned sales stuff in their discourse. Funny business (sometimes called bullshit) is palpable. It's kind of like the politician who said he couldn't define pornography, but he knows it when he sees it. Serving people is about them, not your agenda. I like it when people help me and care for me.

Value proposition? This will be dealt with in later chapters. These repeated phrases kind of rub me the wrong way. Just sayin'.

This is the overall mindset I have chosen to follow for the majority of my life. Whenever I have strayed from this, failure is just around the corner. There have been plenty of failures. There have been ten times more successes. I hope that in the final analysis, I will be remembered for my tenacity and growth and the belief that I can do better. The way I see it, if I live to be a hundred (possible in my mind, but there will need to be a lot of replacement parts by then), and if five to ten years didn't go well, at least it will still be possible to get an A in the class.

I'll go into how I became me in the following chapters, but it doesn't really matter. You became you in the same manner. You were born, and you had an upbringing to endure. Hopefully, you were loved (I love you, by the way... for real), and you feel ready to take on the task of providing for the family through your service (& sales.) If at any point you feel like my words could help you or your team grow, please feel free to reach out and ask. My job is to serve others and to pay it all forward.

People were generally friendly to me, for many reasons and nicer at some points in my life than others. That is partly why I know that serving others works. Most people are less selfish than they may seem on the surface. People like to help and to be helped. To serve and to be served.

What do I remember the most from my upbringing? The nice stuff. The fun stuff. It's that simple. And really, that made it easier for me to be excellent. Then things are more fun. Whenever I dwell on the negative parts, I stop having fun. At some point, everyone realizes we have one lifetime (maybe some would object), so let's focus on the positives.

The Positive Scale – When I visualize positives and negatives, I see a scale with a glass bowl on each side. When a negative gets tossed in the bowl on the right, it takes ten positives in the left bowl to create a balanced scale. Was the glass bowl you visualized clear? The negatives are in a clear glass bowl. The positives are in one of Grandma 1950's aqua-colored glass bowls. Negatives weigh ten times more, and we stare at them to our demise. We don't like the negative, but we can't stop staring at it. If we keep filling the cheerful bowl, Grandma will make us chocolate chip cookies. We like cookies; now we feel much better. (Note: Please don't use food as a comforting tool, but you get the idea.) And now, what if we change the bowl color from clear on the negatives, for heaven's sake, so we aren't constantly staring at them (maybe throw them in a garbage bag or freeze them?)

Some of you will have more of an uphill path. Maybe people treated you poorly, abused you, or didn't value you. I want to pause here to say how sorry I am about these things that have happened to you. I am deeply and truly sad. I wish you hadn't been treated the way you were treated, and I hope everyone would just be friendly to you, always. You are 1000 times more valuable than any diamond. You have made a massive difference in the world just by being you. And you have unlimited potential to grow past anything. You will grow past everything.

I am here for you, doing what I do if you were to need anything. I hope that what I am able to do for you contributes somehow to your success and, at a minimum, makes you more hopeful and gives you more faith in human beings. We really need each other. And we are starved for kindness.

Success is like baklava. This is a book that drills down on things pertaining to sales and service. For example. Success is when preparation meets opportunity; many people talk about this in sales and motivational genres. I memorized this one when I was nineteen years old, working at Jay Jacobs clothing store. I was the top-selling agent out of over 150 stores for many months. Yes. Success=Preparation+Opportunity. But it's deeper than this. Everyone defines success differently, depending on family, friends, money, career, or many other components. It strikes me that success is more like baklava. Many layers are tough to make properly very time-consuming, and yet, it can be so sweet when it is done with care. Beware, there are nuts (allergy alert! Be advised...) that can cause success to veer off course. But once we taste success, we want more. And that is the magic potion that drives us to serve (& sell.) Also, who would have known it has a Mongolian root word, Layla, meaning to tie up, wrap up, and pile up? I can think of quite a few things that pile up and are far less delicious than baklava. We succeed when we tie up the loose ends, and we are serving when we wrap it all up and give it to others. It makes others feel good when we give them baklava (I do love desserts...)

So, my definition of success went deeper. One day, I was able to listen to a Navy Seal gentleman named Chad Wright talk. His demeanor was chill, seemed almost like a hippie or 70's phase of Forest Gump, and was amazingly captivating. But this is an *intensely intense* man. Determined? His name could be in the dictionary for this word.

In essence, his point sunk deep into my psyche that day (he runs and wins 250k ultra marathons in his spare time.) *It is Adversity that helps complete the equation.* **Success=(Preparation+Opportunity) x Adversity**. We have to be prepared and pursue opportunities, but we must embrace *adversity* first and foremost. We must be expecting it, visualize it before it comes, and welcome it when it does come. We must serve the adversity as though it is a main character in our play. It may seem counterintuitive, but still, it is true. It will always be true. We will be faced with rigorous days, difficult obstacles, and mean people. It's all part of the process of service. But we are serving both ourselves and those around us when we respond with kindness. It is how we respond to things that matter. Adversity requires a kind mindset.

Whether we are selling, helping a woman across the street, washing dishes, scrubbing toilets, doing laundry, getting shots, taking out the garbage, or any number of items that lack the glamour of a salesperson on a mission to sell something (another long run-on sentence, sorry), we do a much better job of it all when we have a service mindset. So, hopefully, this book will help you enjoy selling. Carpe Beneficium!

Chapter 2

Foundation and Bones

By looking at the world we live in, it is easy to see how important structure is to our daily lives. We live in a structure, we shop in structures, we are educated in structures, and we even plan our entire transportation system around structures. Every building was once not there. When we fly above the earth at 35,000 feet and see how little of this place has structure, we start to get it. We are small, and this world is massive—there is a ton to learn here. Let's dig in further...

We structure our lives, our days, our plans, our education, our family life, and almost everything. Structure is a pretty big deal. The bigger deal is the foundation of the structure. All of the previously listed structures have foundational elements. There is always some bearing ground for physical structures to rest upon, and when done correctly, things stay straight and justified for decades and centuries to come.

There are many parallels between construction, service, and sales. The foundation is the most critical component. Everything we build is taught (and therefore learn) and cobbled together on top of the foundation of our lives. In construction, the process of forming the foundation takes time. There is a rebar pattern that needs to match the plans. The engineer decided what was needed and then gave the plans to the construction team. They then read the plan and follow it. The footings are poured first, and then the walls are poured next, using excellent and reputable (proven) concrete. Remove any air pockets with vibration, make sure the top side is smooth and level, and then let it dry. It seems pretty straightforward, and in all reality, it is.

Then things get a bit wonky. Years go by, and though it is the same foundation you've always had, we are often unsure of how this blur of events all led up to right now. Do we have to accept our place in life the way it is? And is it possible to reinforce one's foundation decades later? Oh, hell yeah. That's what we call a remodel. That's what we call earthquake retrofitting.

The first home builder I worked with had an astute observation for me one day. "It's just construction. If we mess something up, we can fix it." This always made me feel calmer about the work I was doing when I was learning the home-building trade. What I realized is I should surround myself with contractors who share the same mindset and values, and together, we could build anything. It is no different than being a chef. There are those set norms recipes that have unfolded for thousands of years, the foundation for the craft, and there is the trellis we construct upon the foundation. We are the vine that grows on the trellis. Our efforts every year bear fruit unless someone prunes back our foliage too far. And when this happens, we sprout new vines and new foliage. This is the miraculous part.

The interplay between the earth, the sun, the water, and the roots of this vine can be understood scientifically, and yet there are too many coincidences here. My logical mind finally realizes there is likely something divine behind this whole thing. There is an inter-connectedness that emanates past the foundation, the trellis, the vine and the fruit—service springs from all of it. Love pours out of everything from everyone—some more than others. From serving, we build our reverence for the interconnectedness we share. Our foundation is essential, but not the end all. The bones are crucial. It's what we do with the bones that matter.

Sometimes, we have an earthquake, and our being is moved from its foundation. Why didn't we follow our best practices and prepare for the eventuality? What if we retrofit before the earthquake happens? We stay safe. We are in control. We were proactive and planned for the event. We hold tightly to the truth at all times, and we honestly attack the frontier we face. We can put fear aside because we have already visualized this day and knew that service would get us through the toughest of times. Having stayed safe ourselves, we are then able to help others. Serve others. Connect other people with what they need. This is what makes selling from a service mindset feel excellent. Your stock as a person just went up because you were available to help in a disaster. It isn't selling when people see you are able to help, are willing to help, and trust you. They hitch their covered wagon to your train, and they will follow you. Do not lead them astray. Integrity is the key. You can either test if this is true yourself or trust me on this one. Learn from all of us who have tested this already. Trust is your superpower.

For all of this we see around us, the birds, the trees, the clouds, the beautiful sun, the river, the ocean, the & babies, the struggle to survive and then actually surviving, there must be something, or some force helping orchestrate all this. But the mindset is the final frontier. How do we prepare ourselves to notice each other in the day? If everyone we meet and deal with were the same, it would be easy. That is the problem. Nobody is the same. People share similar values, religions, language, traits, and so on, but nobody is the same. And more so, the situation of their upbringing holds the keys to how many obstacles need to be hurdled. Remember, there is only a finite amount. You can hurdle them all. In another chapter, I discuss the chameleon; this is just a heads-up. *So we find our mindset, we breathe in the day, and we forge forward.*

Going back to the whole foundation analogy, some architects and engineers certified the plan actually works to endure the forces of nature that want to pull it apart. But who is the engineer in your life? That's a deep one. Who chose how to pour your foundation? How did we end up with bones that allow us to sit up straight in a chair, jump backward over a six-foot bar (did this one) or carry materials from here to there? While we likely can't answer these questions, it is worth pondering.

Because our design is unique to each of us, we benefit from understanding the extrinsic ingredients that helped form us. For many, how their upbringing affected their foundation is all a big blur. Memories versus perceptions is a vast topic (for another time), but it will affect how we serve others. How did we develop to be a positive-minded or negative-minded person? Did we ever have a choice? Do we have an option right now to change our mindset? How far back have we looked at our history to understand where things took a turn and how we then responded to those turns? Ask yourself, "What was my mindset at those critical times...?" Get it out of your system, and record it on paper. Knowing what you know now, how will you address your mindset to help you increase your ability to serve (& sell) more effectively?

I have read many sales books and even had a chance to help outline one for another well-known personality. Each person who achieves notoriety or rises to the top of their trade has their recipe for how they did it and how they think you should or could do it. This stuff isn't rocket science or even brain surgery (I've been there, no fun...). It's actually more complex than these in many ways. Service and sales take everything you have ever learned and expose it. This begs the question, why would anyone want to stop learning (another book.) Service exposes who you are. The type of person you are, your past, your skills, your interests, and the kind of person you are striving to be. It is all on display. Unlike acting, it isn't a script that somebody else wrote for you, and you then get to memorize it. No, in this case, it is you, being you, in an improv situation. For money. Now.

When we reduce it to this simple concept, it starts to be clear that we should be on stage as much as possible if we want to get the Oscar someday. Some of the sales gurus already have an Oscar (metaphorically speaking, kind of...). I'm not in sales for the awards. I want to help make the world a better place. And if I am successful financially, I will be better suited to achieve my true potential. What is the limit? There is no limit. How much does it pay? Unlike nearly everything else, there is no limit. Sales are a miracle. So why isn't everyone selling? Many people are, trust me. But it is those who have the service mindset that are killing it.

So a guy asked me one day as I was knocking on doors, "So you just drop by homes, strike up conversations, find something awry with my budget, save me over $150K over the next twenty-five years, and walk away with a $5000 check? In a matter of an hour or two?" Pretty much. Yeah, that's what we do. He will have no power bill in the next five years, and he is in control. He converted an accounting liability into an ever-rising asset with one decision. He will change his net worth by hundreds of thousands over the next 20 years with the click of a DocuSign. That's about it. Maybe I should stop the book right here... Nah.

We turn inward to our memories, and we bring them out. However, curiosity about the other person is how it starts. We help the client tap into their memories and what makes them feel good, and we care. We are kind. A distilled version of the service mindset could be described as an energetic and empathetic desire to help people tap into what makes them feel good. Do not sell people. But help people.

Marsha Sinetar wrote a great book (well, a ton of great books) about tapping into what drives us. *Do What You Love, The Money Will Follow.* She doesn't mention how much money will follow, and that is a point of contention that many starving artists and self-oriented salespeople share, but regardless, follow your passion. Service will get you to your goals. Goals? This is another chapter, but it needs to be addressed. Avoid burning down your future by setting and sticking to the goals you deem critical to your future.

How do we do it? There isn't a set recipe, but it can be deciphered for each person quickly. On a piece of paper, draw a line vertically down the center, and on the left top, write "Favorite Things," and you guessed it, on the right, "Least Favorite Things." So, these favorites are part of our foundation. These least favorites are also part of our foundation. Put subjects in school, hobbies, cars, houses, people, church, animals, mean spirits, sports, weather, exercise, leaders, anything you want, on either side. This is a mind dump. On my own, I would have "learning" as a favorite, which ties back to curiosity, which ties to everything, including service (& sales). It's only later in life that I figure out "teaching" is just as key to me as "learning." And they say, if you want to learn something better, try to teach it (which is all a tiny glimpse into my brain and choices I have made.)

In sales, we are educators. But first and foremost, we are also micro-historians or maybe wanna-be autobiographers. We want to find out the history of the life of the person we are talking with to understand better how to help them solve their problem.

And after we dump it all onto a page or pages, we go back to the positives column ten times more often than to the negatives. We are beginning the process of changing the weight of our thought processes first. Ten times the positives, once in a while the negatives. Repeat this day after day. How do the negatives make you feel when you apply thought to them? How do the positives make you feel? If you're anything like me, you probably want a life filled with positives. You want to feel good. And when you feel good, you are ready to serve.

But you may ask, "How do we drill down on the recipe for how to structure or formulate our life? And how will that make us money?" Great question. Your curiosity and our desire to bring you along for the ride so you can see this process in action is what unfolds in this book.

How will that make us money, as much as possible, in the shortest amount of time? That's the subtext of the question above from most young salespeople we encounter in the field. While it is a great question, it is a question to ask later. One of the first questions is, "How can I serve you?" But even this is not the first question.

In sales, you usually know how you are trying to serve the person in your field. If they show up on a car lot, for example, you know they were attracted to the lot through some means, and they are now standing in front of you. But even earlier than that, as they approach you, a thought pops into your head (this is organic, impromptu sales at work), and this is the first question. "Wow, that's a good-looking posse; how old are these kids." It seems cheesy, but do it from your voice and heart, in the moment, impromptu, and genuinely care about the person and the answer they will give. It all starts with this. "I've got a few of my own at home" may be your next move after they answer. And that's enough about you. Back to their kids, their purse, their smile, something endearing. But your job is to wait for an answer first. Maybe they are there to look at cars. Perhaps they have a daughter graduating college, and they want to purchase a new vehicle for her. You never know what the intent or situation is for anyone you meet. But genuine, familiar, everyday dialogue is a great starting point. The whole point is this day, this moment, and this experience is all about them, not you. It's about kindness. It's about caring. It's about positives.

Become great at impromptu conversations and know your stuff. Become great at noticing what is essential to people. Study things every day. What is in the news? What is the history of the neighborhood you are selling in? What is new in the industry and trends? What is new about our product, and why is this the perfect time to consider our product? If the people in sales are going to be paid like doctors, then it is also imperative to bring the same level of curiosity, study, learning, and caring that a doctor would bring. Sales is a privilege. Not everyone is suited for it, but most of us actually are suited for it. Or at least, we can remodel our mindset and become better suited for it. Like everything else, service (& sales) is a learned craft.

It starts with the foundation. This house has good bones. Let's do a remodel; it's time to change things up a bit. It's time to grow. We all yearn for growth. We all desire to serve others.

Chapter 3

Service Above Self

Love Others, Get Stuff Done!

*W*hat's in it for me? (One writer calls this the radio channel, WIIFM). When you hear the phrase, know you're on a slippery slope and probably on the wrong track. Technically, we are still focusing on the foundation here. The mindset you bring to the service (& sales) you pursue is critical to your success. *If you know that you tend toward the "me, me, me..." then this is your chance to learn the "we, we, we."* (That should be a song or a dance.) It is more fun to dance with others than to do it yourself, after all. The three little pigs did it together, and then we went all the way home.

We have been steeped for the past several decades in a tea that is getting more and more bitter. I know there are also a ton of great things happening. I could list them all here, but you could likely look back at the list you already made of Favorites and Least Favorites to see if you need to add anything else to the list. When you think of the world we live in through this prism, one of selfish consumerism, where your wants outweigh your needs, it all starts to make more sense. Take a minute to update the list. Then, progress to the following list. *Are you satisfied or frustrated with your situation?*

Think of today as an example. Maybe yesterday and the day before, or perhaps even a whole week, so that you can understand patterns each week. You remember these days fairly closely (if you didn't alter your mind much) because they just happened. What did you love about the last few days, and what do you wish had gone better?

For me, the last few days have been both satisfying and frustrating. So, the question is, how can I increase satisfaction and decrease frustration? Not too harsh in hindsight. But how do we convert hindsight to foresight? This is where our focus needs to lie. I am suggesting a logbook, almost like a daily diary, dedicated to **Satisfying** (first half of the journal) and **Frustrating** (second half of the journal.) Write the list before bed each night instead of staring at the screen. It's easy to keep it updated this way.

The goal may be to fill the satisfying half of the journal before the frustrating half. If we are focused on seeking positives, they will outweigh our negatives, and we will be living life with intent. We can relate this to service (& sales) in the coming pages and chapters; hold this thought (or highlight this concept) at the front of your mind for right now.

It's a relatively simple concept, but the real work is in just making it happen. Get stuff done. Make sure it is more in the Satisfying column than the Frustrating column. You are able to make choices each day, so why wait another day? If you don't have or can't afford a logbook, make one out of old papers and staple them together. I have an idea. If they already have writing on them, then use a Sharpie and write over the top of the old stuff. Be inventive, be creative. Just start to make things happen.

Satisfying (past few days) –

- I got the kitchen looking clean before bed so that the morning would be mentally calm (this is especially important to my wife, so I count this as "service above self.")
- Read a great NY Times article about how Taylor Swift's art, words, music, demeanor, and mindset are having a positive effect on the psychology of an entire generation. Fascinating stuff here. Every day, I find great articles, and they provide a theme for my mind to hold closely for a day or so...
- Made coffee for my "home from college" daughter. Although she wanted fresh ground coffee, we only had Folgers instant, which I have developed a taste for (and is super cheap.) So, this is an opportunity to serve better in the coming days. Although I did ask her if she wanted some instant hot chocolate in it, too, such as homemade mocha, she declined (trying to exceed her expectations).
- I went to church (I have been at the same Catholic church for 57 years, a source of comfort in my life.) My parents got married there. They divorced 17 years later, so that happened.
- I listened to some new music on the way to church, as well as a few oldies, including a theme from Rocky.
- Went on a short walk with my blind golden retriever. She's only three years old and has glaucoma, but she is coping well and stays happy. This dog inspires me. She has a fantastic mindset for the most part and doesn't complain when she runs into large rocks and walls and things. She shakes it off, and I try to learn to help her avoid this eventuality better each day.

- I am focused on solar sales and the new automated solar panel cleaning system, which has thrown my sales life into overdrive. There is no end to the amount of energy I could pour into this product and solar power. Everyone with Solar needs it (only 3-4% of Americans so far), and everyone who will be buying Solar needs this system included (for no additional money.) I could spend another book writing about case studies and how this is a massively disruptive technology, but that's enough for now (and welcome people to reach out about it...)
- I had a meeting with Walmart, and it went very well.
- I spent time helping to build a new sales company. I am part of a team that is revolutionizing how Clean Solar and Clean Batteries will be the next phase of the puzzle. Goal: Bring generational power to disadvantaged and blue-collar consumers—end power bills.
- I watched two of my daughters do great at their swim meet.
- We had a picnic at the beach with my wife and daughter while looking at Mount Rainier on a pleasant June evening. We had homemade cheese biscuits and a fantastic basil-mint tomato snap pea salad. My wife is a great cook; we love food.
- We recruited three new people to be part of the team.
- Helped several new homeowners convert to Solar, thus getting a power bill with no inflation and en route to no power bill in the future.
- Sang at the top of my lungs with my daughter on a car ride back from church.
- I laughed with each of my children, my brother and his family, and my wife at a family gathering. We love to laugh.

- I made lunch for my daughter, then did the dishes together while listening to "Food Glorious Food" from Oliver.
- They made lists of areas to focus on in the coming days, weeks, months and years.
- I had my in-grown toenails fixed after a year of bothering me. They haven't been healing correctly due to the medicine I have to take as a result of the Valley Fever I contracted while doing the work I do... (a story for another time.) This is something to avoid, trust me.
- I wrote in my book about sales (the one you're reading.) I find that writing a chapter a day is a good goal when I am in the mood to write. Some weeks, it isn't doable, and I tend to take some months free of writing to gather momentum.
- I visualized helping four new people convert over to Solar this coming week. On average, this week of service (&sales) will save four families a total of a half-million dollars over the coming two decades.
- I helped my mother-in-law sell her Dacor range. I realize I have a knack for this kind of thing, and it's something I know how to do.
- Wrote a song.
- Wrote two poems.
- I watched my brother's orchestra play at an outdoor park.
- I had an indoor rainy-day picnic at my other brother's place.
- Frustrating (past few days...)
- I changed my Valley Fever medicine. It has some frustrating side effects, such as flashing light in my eyes and gut ache, but putting them out of my mind. Doing things makes frustrations go away.
- I got more medical bills in the mail.

- I didn't get the paycheck I was supposed to get for the 2nd week in a row.
- I had to skip two days of writing in the book.
- Motor going out on the mini-van.
- Didn't work out.
- I left the kitchen messy one day for my wife to come home to. I was running kids around, and working sometimes got tricky.
- I haven't done the yard maintenance in weeks.
- I couldn't drive two hours to see my mom like I wanted to, so I ran out of time.
- Didn't hit my sales goal this past week. Diligence and tenacity are a "must" this coming week.
- A deal fell through (which is an immediate invitation to attack sales...)
- Prospecting was on the back burner; I need it on the front.

So it looks like this, day after day, for years and years. It's called life. The question is, how do we move more of the frustrations to the satisfaction heading?

The short answer involves working smarter. And beyond this, the longer answer takes a whole book to unfold. More accurately, it takes an entire life to unfold. But this process of spreading the tablecloth over the table of our life always involves just getting stuff done.

What are the things that hold us back from getting things done? This is another list.... Write it down for yourself, but see if some of these things end up on your list. I'm sure you'll come up with tons of other things. Feel free to send me emails at josephdevine@ mail.com (no attachments), chronicling a paragraph or two of things that keep you from getting stuff done. If it's more than two pages, I won't have time to read it.

- Health issues
- Training
- I have to work too much.
- In a dead-end job
- I don't love what I do.
- Too tired
- Weather
- It takes too much work to work more.
- A mind preoccupied with problems.
- Relationship issues
- In an unhealthy living environment
- Don't have enough money to make ends meet.
- Transportation issues
- Am too sad

These are the things that hold us back. These are the things that end up hobbling us. They are our excuses. We use these to keep things the same. And if we keep them the same, we won't be able to get out of the loop. I would be happy to hear some of yours. Sometimes, all we need is a sounding board, and the next move on the chessboard of our lives appears. Again, like magic.

With some of these, we don't have choices because they just are. These things happen to us. Here is the deeper magic to service (& sales) that few people realize. It is how we respond to the things that hold us back that determines whether and how we can put these things behind us. It is our mindset that delivers us to the next level.

Imagine life as a 100-floor building. So far, we have gotten to know all the floors up to our age. We don't get to progress to the next level until our birthday. But what if years were only half years? What if our life is just a half-life? I'm sure you've met people who seem wise beyond their years. Many people refer to the "old souls" when describing someone. Fully explore at every floor.

I play basketball. I love basketball. I'm pretty good at basketball, but certainly not great. My first year being allowed to be on a team was in seventh grade. The fundamentals were the central part that vexed me. Everyone on the team was much further ahead of me. But luckily, I was athletic. It always takes a little luck on things; being athletic was lucky. So early on, I decided to practice plenty, and I knew that if I tried a little harder than everyone else on the team, the coach would notice.

I used this same strategy for the next five years. Some people had better skills that maybe should have made the team in each of the years. Yet slowly, one year at a time, my hard work and strategy proved to work. Work works. I played varsity basketball in my senior year. I certainly didn't get to play in the games much. But when the coach would put me in, I was a spectacle. Now imagine a cow dog that hasn't been with the cattle for many days. Herding the cattle is part of the dog's DNA. Defense was my superpower and was in my DNA. I didn't want to let my man score or even dribble to his dominant-hand side. Ever.

The way I was able to serve my team was through sheer effort— service above self. The team is what mattered. And remembering back, my teammates and coach always did appreciate that about me. For the decades after high school, my game actually did improve, and I was able to learn about how to work smarter, not harder. But still, the mindset I had drilled into my being was always going to be there. If I focus on performing for the good of the team by serving my clients, I would naturally reap the benefits myself. And it felt better to me.

So, if I put in more effort than others, it stands to reason that my successes will grow faster than those of others. The half-life concept is born from this reality. Those who 'get stuff done' are the engine that drives business. At times, it feels as though I have lived two lives. The number of experiences I have had boggle my mind when I look back.

How can this happen? To understand this, ask yourself what things you spend time on that are distracting your ability to get more stuff done. Below are a few of the things on many people's lists:

- Screens (What good does this do me? Can I reduce it weekly?)
- Complaining (What good does this do me? Can I reduce it weekly?)
- Alcohol (probably the top of the list and the one most people are in denial about)
- Drugs (Why do drugs when so many don't need to? When was I drug-free?)
- Distraction (What is easy for me to focus on? Should I work in that field?)
- Talking too much (Why not listen more?)
- Negativity (Why be negative?)
- Tiredness (Why am I so tired?)
- Kids (Yes, and do they give me joy? Why did I have them? What is most important?)
- Parents (Is there a way to embrace this time with my parents, making it crucial to growth?)
- Friends (What am I doing with my friends? Are these friends good for me?)
- Pets (Am I in a position to have a pet and give it the time and care it needs?)

Circle this whole group of headings or highlight the ones that are vexing you. How are you able to work on these, make the time you spend each day part of the Satisfaction column, and remove it from the Frustration column? Service above self, yes. But who is the first person we should serve before being able to serve others fully? And does this make us selfish? Not if you then use your more centered mindset and being to serve others, then more effectively.

You've heard the saying, "You must love yourself before you are able to love others." This is a truism. But it takes practice first. It is best to work on your skills and know your shortcomings before working to help people in the world.

Raise your hand if you love excellent service. Raise your hand if you are in love with a partner that knows how to service you. OK, don't let your mind go too far down this path, but in general, aren't the best relationships the ones where one person wants to serve the other? If we want a network of relationships in our business and sales lives, then why would we not apply this same principle to our daily work? Our daily work is what we have chosen to do with our days on this planet. How many days will we have on the earth? None of us really knows, but maybe the better question is, should we waste any of them? Time is of the essence. Let's get it.

Chapter 4

Flesh

The "There" There

W e yearn for the fruit. We need the wood, the roots, and the stalk for various parts of sustenance, but we yearn for the fruit. The fruit is the flesh. Meat is also flesh. How do we find the flesh of the service we give? The flesh of the sale is the byproduct of the hard work.

Imagine you are a farmer. Or, imagine you are a hunter. Either way, you are working to make strides toward having a crop or meal to harvest. What does life feel like each day if you are a farmer? My family clan spans four hundred years in North America. And thousands of years before this in Europe. Also, there are parts of the family that are descendants of Native American life. These relatives also lived off the land and in nature.

It feels unique to be from a culture of both cowboys and Indians (Native Americans, but I use the word Indians to illustrate how I was brought up.) As kids, we played Cowboys and Indians on our horses. We lived the white privilege lifestyle because our cowboy father became a horse doctor. But our mother lived the same way. Her Native American descent father pulled himself through a dust bowl of Oklahoma and Texas childhood and headed west toward different pastures and different opportunities. His effort achieved a unique result. He was great with horses and thus was able to teach the children of the well-to-do how to be part of the horse world. He would teach them how to be hunter-jumper contestants, therefore coaching and guiding them to a life they would have otherwise never known.

Isn't it true we are all seeking something to pull us out of our everyday situations and deliver us to something more fulfilling? Yes, some have already been delivered. But this seems to be the exception to the rule. On average, almost all of us wish our lives could be better somehow.

You are cracking the code by reading this book. Again, it isn't rocket science, but it is instead both an art and a science to navigate the world of changing a mindset. Having done the work multiple times to address and change my perspective, I feel compelled to pass on what I have learned. I don't want anyone to think I am an expert at anything, nor do I want others to think my mindset is better than theirs. I want to help people find a better mindset for themselves.

The flesh of service (& sales) is an unyielding belief that our efforts, our work, can be the fruit that sustains our bodies and minds in a way that then makes us grow more quickly than we would have imagined and helps those around us do the same, and finally helps us all to achieve better results than we ever thought possible. Synergistic results are the byproduct of getting stuff done. When we subscribe to a belief that learning is growing, then we grow. When we join a class or a team, then we grow. When we do art, write books or poetry, or read, then we grow. When we play or watch sports together, then we grow. When we cook a meal together, then we grow. We are the anatomy of service (& therefore sales.) We are the common denominator. "We the people..." is a concept that will live on far beyond when we read this book or when I thought it should be written.

The bones and foundations are the foundations upon which flesh rests. We become the meat on the bones of service. If it weren't for us all, there would be no service and no need for service.

This is a service economy. How do we add value to the sales we are pursuing and to the products we are representing? The main ingredient and manner in which we become critical to our customers is by providing better service. It doesn't matter if we make the sale. It never does. But guess what? We will make the sale through fantastic service. We will get our clients to talk about us to their friends. They will say things like, "This person is the real deal!" We are the sweet fruit that they will pick when deciding which apple to choose at the market. We are the excellent apple.

What is the Flesh? You've heard people ask, "Where is the there, there?" Or maybe, "There is no there, there." Interesting concept, I agree. But what it really means is, "Where is the meat on the bones of this story?"

The flesh of this book relates to the human story. People drive sales. Caring about people and seeing them as important people in the world is the number one way to be received warmly when working to help them. If you are trying to sell them and not serve them, then maybe change the fields. Should we sell things or services that are not helpful to others? Nope.

Are you in a field that helps others or hurts others? If it is the latter, change fields at this point, then start rereading this book after you have done so. I love what I do, and I wouldn't change it for something that helps people less. But if I could find a field that even helps people more, then heck yeah, I would make the change. Or, at a minimum, work to incorporate this new field into my daily routine of service (& sales.)

Isn't it exciting to realize that you can do anything in any field if you dig into the field of work and start working? Just get stuff done. That is the "Flesh" of what it means to serve others. Again, Get Stuff Done!

And make sure the stuff you do is helping, not hurting.

Let's go!

How do I make a change? Making a change to one's diet or the flesh we decide to consume to sustain us isn't always as easy as it is made out to be. Yet, additionally, it isn't as tricky as we allow ourselves to make it out to be.

Another list... If I could do anything today to help others, what field would I want it to be in?

Make a list, with the right side of the page being "In an Ideal World..." On the left side of the piece of paper, write "Current world..."

In an ideal world...

- I wouldn't have to work at all. (Then do what you love; you won't work a day in your life!)
- I would work about 3-4 hours per day. (Then, if that's what you want, let's do it!)
- I would read the book "The Four-Hour Work Week" and figure out how to work even less.
- I would get caught up less on how much I work and more on "How much can I achieve that helps change the world?"

- I would have more money in the bank. (Then let's set the right goals to achieve this.)
- I would travel more. (What if travel were part of your work?)
- I would find ways to enjoy work. (This starts with nurture from parents at a young age. Read Steven Covey and see if you can figure out what the acronym Dr. Grac stands for. Hint: highly effective people book...) Stewardship is the key.
- I would stay in better shape. (Start small, stretching, then do 4-5 minutes more each day. Soon you will OWN your health...Unless there is a deeper issue you were born with or are enduring from an accident. Regardless, we can grow in our health just a touch each day if we try...)
- I would eat better. (You can.)
- I would spend more time with my family. (Please start today. Play a game with your daughter, grandparent, or parent. If you have none of these, call a distant relative. Please grow!)
- I would learn more and take classes that would help me grow.

There is no end to this list. You can keep going daily to find your answers. I will let you make a list of your current world. But make it at least as robust as your "Ideal" world... Isn't it great how our mindset can be molded? We can focus on the things that make life better, starting today.

Again, start now. Get stuff done. Have a body of work. **Be Prolific in order to Be.**

Chapter 5

Oxygen and Blood

Smooth Systems and Operations

Why do you feel good on the days when you feel good? What do you need more of on the days you don't feel good? How is "good" defined in our minds?

"How are you doing today? Pretty good. How are you?"

The fundamental question for one another each day is so simple. And this same question is very complicated.

The anatomy of the human body is often reduced to parts, bone names, physical attributes, colors, sizes, muscles, and even down to the smallest cells. All of these parts work together to help the body operate on a level that is reasonably automated when nothing is going awry. But when things aren't going well, we tend to focus on the malfunctioning parts. We talk about these parts and pains and tend to use them as excuses for why we aren't quite up to snuff (which means "not good.")

Even when we aren't up to snuff, we are taught to talk about ourselves as being "pretty good." "*Accentuate the positives, elimi-nate the negatives*" is how the lyrics go on the song of our lives. In many ways, this tendency to want to mitigate the negatives actually works. Yet, we don't talk about the more profound complexity of how the body interacts with the environment as much.

I have asthma and am used to not getting enough oxygen in my system at various times.

The low-grade anxiety this causes makes it difficult to be "pretty good." One of the only solutions is to get used to it.

Also, since I was a small child, my blood has tended to be a bit anemic. I was prescribed iron pills when I was young, but I stopped taking them the older I got. Even when I've had my blood taken in adulthood, my blood has continued to lack all the minerals needed to be healthy. But I've gotten used to it. Most everyone has ailments that have become the background noise of their lives. The tendency is to "get used to it."

So, we all have our shortcomings, challenges, and issues to contend with. We need oxygen, and we need blood. And even when our condition threatens these, our bodies will try to compensate and keep going. The machine of our bodies is borderline miraculous. OK, actually, a miracle. How do things that pull us down also keep us alive? How do we contend with all the downfalls while at the same time living a functional life? If our body is a temple, and it is always in interaction with the world around us, how is it possible for us to improve our situation as the years progress?

Adaptation is part one of the short answers to the question of survival. The mind adapts to its situation. And when that happens, the body usually follows suit. *Modern medicine* and a holistic approach to health can also be part of that short answer and is part two for many of us. If it weren't for both of these, a constant state of degradation would have a more powerful effect on our lives, and it would be tough to grow and improve as the years progress. From the day we are born, we are on a path toward death. Sadly, this very fact can overwhelm some minds. But does it have to? I'm pretty sure the answer is overwhelmingly "no." We don't have to succumb to the conditions we are exposed to or are born with; and instead, we can adapt to them. We can overcome almost anything through mindset.

Once we learn how to cope with our situation, we tend to keep surviving and are even able to learn to thrive. We cope with body and mind and with the environment that allows these to exist. Oxygen and blood will enable us to exist in the first place. Thank heavens for this. So why do we tear ourselves down? Why do we allow our minds to degrade? Why do we allow ourselves to be beaten when things get tough? The fact is, not all of us do allow ourselves to be beaten. Some will survive and even thrive, while others will accept their situation and allow it to defeat them. *Survival of the fittest* is part three of the equation. When we keep our bodies and minds fit, we are ready for smooth operations to occur. You might be asking, "How can I get the mindset to be one of the survivors?" Loving the others is how I believe it is achieved.

If you've ever spent time watching the show "Survivor," you may learn it is best to be one of the characters of love in the play of life. Many of us are victims of our situation. It's when we move past being a victim and start sharing love we begin to become the person we want to be. The survivor mindset is also one of back-biting. Dog eat dog world. "I will survive at all costs." And then what? It's only you? You survived, but at the cost of relationships and by causing pain for others? Ah, hell no... Keep moving, yes. But put the difficulties of the past behind you.

Move the frustrating parts of your life to the satisfying column. Learn from when you were defeated. Embrace the adversity, and share yourself with others. We can all grow from your experiences.

We are the oxygen and blood for one another. We need each other. Oxygen and blood unite us. When we go through challenging situations, we sometimes ask, "Why me?" But we are united by difficult situations and by our condition. We all process the oxygen differently, and all our blood that carries the oxygen has its unique characteristics. This is part of being an individual. We identify with one another because we are all human. But some identify with humans better than others. Some carry hatred in their oxygen, which then affects their being and mindset. We are certainly different than one another. We have distinct histories. Why were we born, when and where are we in this world? Luck? Maybe. Because we were born into our situation, we all have a different sense of home.

We long for people, for like-minded people. But the likeness of mind has to be discovered for ourselves, on our own. Then, we need to share it with others. We all need oxygen. We all need blood. We can become both for each other.

Finding Ourselves – The baby must separate from the mother at some point. When this doesn't happen, there tend to be blurred boundaries. Instead of seeing our truth and living the life we were born to live, we sometimes mimic others and do things for others for the wrong reasons. Why should we serve others? Because for most of us, it makes us feel good. Then things get confusing. We are trying to find ourselves and figure out how we are supposed to serve the world at large. Unfortunately, we sometimes go about it the wrong way.

It is true most of us long for places where there are people. We want to belong to something, so we try to find our niche or our group that seems the same as us. We may look in magazines and see ourselves in others. If we don't like what is in the magazine, we grab a different kind of magazine. There must be a better way. There is a recipe for our growth.

While knocking on doors over the years to convey how Solar can save people a ton of money, we have noticed that people who like their neighbors are a great place to expand their solar footprint. If people don't want one another in a neighborhood, they tend to all get more negative, thus making the sale more challenging.

Sometimes, we are searching for a better version of ourselves, but we focus on the wrong things. We believe that some picture of our perfect life is out there. We grab different magazines, watch other shows, or find new friends in order to find ourselves. This is dangerous because it sometimes brings people to gangs, cults, and political parties and further away from their best selves. We feel misunderstood, so we go find a place where people identify with us or understand us. The problem usually is that we have not yet seen how to serve others. People who seek love from a different group often have not yet spent the time necessary to be understood by their current family or friends.

Feel free to be you. And if others won't embrace the "you" you want to be, talk about it or make a change. This involves building trust. This consists of building bridges. The thriver outlives the survivor. Growing is tantamount to thriving. Resilience is a prerequisite to surviving. So what if we are resilient and would thrive through service? Can this be a recipe for becoming a product that sells? Are we a product that bears fruit and feeds others?

Whether the situation we find ourselves in is good for us or unhealthy for us, we can usually improve it through service. Becoming a giver is a powerful way to heal. The giver will prosper. Becoming a forgiver is the ultimate way to heal.

Once we have learned to heal and self-soothe ourselves, we have been filled with enough love to then take our pitcher of love around to others and pour them a cup of ourselves. The following prerequisite to becoming someone who can improve their situation is to make sure that you're working to love yourself nonstop.

Are you in a magazine already, ready to be shared with others? Probably not in the sense that someone has written about us and shared images of us so that our story will become part of what feeds the next person. But maybe someday you will be because other people will want to be like you. We don't want to be Mike. We want to be "like Mike." We strive to become better at what we do. Hopefully, this is through service because there is no greater calling.

In a way, this means that our life is metaphorically the images and story in a magazine already. Go with this concept. Serve your talents and skills to others. If you are good at something, go with it. Then, you become great at something, and it gives you a bigger audience to serve. Maybe someone will then write about you.

What if we could all have a larger audience to serve each day? What if our exceptional talent, our oxygen, and our blood, no matter how healthy we are ourselves, could be shared with others to make them more nutritious? Like Mike, we aren't perfect. Even Jordan has his shortcomings. None of us is better than the next. Does it feel better to share and give or to take and consume? Our story is a journey of discovery. Again, does it feel better to share and give or better to take and consume? Seriously, really think about that question. Then, go practice getting better at what you do. Try harder each day. Serve.

How do you want to be remembered? Are you tenacious in the pursuit of service? Are you continuing to learn so you can continue to share what you have learned? We know each other. Learn by listening. If you do become a Master of Service, the top line (sales) of your organization (which is you, yourself) will become larger and larger. Your service (& sales) will determine your success, no matter how you like to measure this success. Selling isn't always easy, but it almost always revolves around a positive mindset of service. And practice your trade relentlessly. Watch and listen to others. Absorb the oxygen that sustains us all. A healthy lifestyle will lead to healthy blood. Which then leads to smooth operations. I love Sade.

You are the lifeblood of a smoothly operating life. You and your mindset are the keys to your effectiveness. Take a deep breath (thank heavens for oxygen) and get in a mindset that allows you to serve your bottom line.

Should I Give Up? When you feel negativity creeping in, remember that it's time to pour in ten times more positively to balance the scale. This is a never-ending task to achieve, this daily privilege (not daily grind... change your mind!) of working toward a positive mindset, and it always proves to increase your sales (legacy) in the end. Your hard work daily will pay off. Be unrelenting (tenacious) about positivity. At the very least, you will feel better "when the head hits the pillow" (I like this saying better than at the end of the day), so your dreams will then fall in line with your consciously *perceived* and *lived* daily life.

PS – Many people identify a glass of wine with the saying, "At the end of the day..." Cloudy dreams hurt feelings, and mayhem is not worth it; the wine causes distance from your immediate life experiences. Liquor is also addictive; little side note here... Stay clean. And the dreams are often too freaky when we aren't clear-headed. Let's cut down on the altered mindset so you can find your best and most positive attitude.

PSS – My wife chose me in 1994 because I had stopped drinking a year earlier. Mostly, good things happened from that point forward. The incredible thing was the fact that we survived seven years of infertility and then went on to have three beautiful and unique children. Doctors helped us achieve the first two. And on April Fools Day 2008, we found out that miracles can happen without the use of doctors as well... In spite of being a non-drinker, there were still some frustrating things that kept creeping up on me (after all, I had already put twelve years of addictive consumption on the board by this point, so I was good at it). Still, at our wedding, we toasted with root beer floats and decided to fight the world together in service of one another and those in our community. Again, desserts feel (and taste) good.

Resolve to feel better, and put a root before your beer. Get addicted to service until you have forgotten the other ways to be. We have been together twenty-nine years, married for twenty-seven of these years. Quitting was always an option, whether it be marriage or drinking. It's better to quit drinking than quitting on a best friend. However, both are possible to leave. The more challenging thing is to stay together sometimes. Continued service to a family is understanding how to put others before yourself. And for some, it's not always possible to commit to hard things. This is OK, but it is certainly worth giving everything one has in the relentless and tenacious pursuit of committing to growth and learning.

Why does it feel so great to think of this family of mine? Why did the idea of never quitting feel better than relenting? I also love Peter Gabriel (Don't Give Up!)

Time to work. I love work.

Chapter 6

Good Ingredients

Know the Recipe! And Choose Ingredients Wisely!

Who besides me loves a great meal? Mostly everyone. Who besides me knows how to prepare and create a great meal? Less than everyone, unfortunately. But as with most everything, if we serve it, they will come.

I remember the feeling of going to my Grandma's house on the farm in Walla Walla when I was a kid. These were my favorite meals of the year for me. Typically, I would spend spring vacation or a good part of the summer on the farm. There was a big garden with all sorts of fruits and vegetables. There was also plenty of work to do first to get to mealtimes.

Grandma spent much of her life feeding farmhands at breakfast and lunchtime. They were on their own for dinner, back to wherever they lived. But there were stories about how some of the workers didn't even worry about dinner because they knew they had a big farm breakfast coming the following day.

Walking up to her home in the morning after being in the field was one of the greatest feelings I can remember. The farm was a ranch where beef and dairy products were raised, and many fruits and vegetables were grown. There were chickens in the barn, which meant there were fresh eggs. Grandma was able to make her butter (although as the years progressed, it was easier to buy it up at Wade's.) The smells of coffee, ripe cantaloupe, sausage on the cooktop and cold butter on warm toast would make me feel great. The birds were awake, the sprinklers ticking in rhythm, and cool air ruffled the sheer curtains, all while laughing and voices drifted to my bed from the kitchen.

Having ingredients that one could pick and be served within one day was such a treat. And it didn't matter how many friends or farmhands there were to serve; Grandma just kept cooking. She smiled the whole time and loved the conversations with all the people who came to her kitchen. We would always try to help with dishes after the meal, but she would insist we rest after eating because there would be plenty of work for everyone to do as the day progressed. "You kids need a cool drink!" she would say. She made lemonade from scratch and would maybe pour a little 7-Up in it when the parents weren't looking. She just wanted us to be happy and didn't really require much of us.

When she did need help, she might ask us to go to the river and see if we could bring back a duck, a teal, or a pheasant. It was miraculous that we were able to go hunting on a farm and pick food from a garden in order to learn how to fend for ourselves.

We helped our uncle and the other farmhands move the sprinklers in the field and learned firsthand how to farm or run a ranch ourselves. We pulled Russian thistles, dozens of acres at a time. We rode ponies through the wheat fields in the week prior to the rye seeding out, cut it off so it wouldn't spread, and put the heads in a gunny sack. We trapped gophers in the asparagus and sweet onion fields. There was no end to the amount of work there was to keep a farm going. Days off weren't really a thing, except for going to church on Sunday. And still, somehow, she made time to bring us to her friends' pool or take us to town for a hand-dipped ice cream cone at DQ. At the County Fair over Labor Day Weekend, she would buy us tickets to each day at the fair while our Dad would rope steers at the Rodeo grounds in the evening. At the end of the weekend, she would fill up our car with ingredients from the farm, frozen meats, and a fresh tank of gas from the tank in the corral and send us on our way to the west. It was sad to leave Grandma's.

I know the concept of service was instilled in me on the farm. Working with Grandma and watching her work was inspirational.

I did well in school and ended up getting a four-year scholarship to the University of Washington for my grades, but after one year of college, I wasn't fulfilled. I didn't know why because I was only nineteen years old at the time, but I decided to take time away from school.

My next move was to have fun dancing at night with friends and explore life on my own. But without money, this quickly came to an end. So I read some books about sales and service and came upon one named *Think and Grow Rich* by Napolean Hill. This one was a mindset changer, thus, a life changer for me.

In essence, the main ingredients I decided to employ in my future were only good ingredients. If fruit should be sweet, then why use bitter fruit in one's life recipe? If it is possible to focus on positives, then why focus on negatives?

So, how would I end up finding what I love to do in order to make money? I landed on the idea of service to others as a training ground. I applied to be a busboy at a local restaurant and was hired. Within a matter of months, the managers loved my attitude and desire to work quickly to such a degree that they taught me how to be a bartender when I turned twenty-one. This was a great job and allowed me to focus on serving people in a manner that built a client base that became like family to me. The clients loved to watch me make drinks because no matter how busy it was to get into the bar, I would not get behind. I was super-fast. This was the same time in history that Tom Cruise did the movie *Cocktail*. I absolutely identified with this character and immersed myself in becoming this memorable bartender.

It was apparent I loved to serve, yet I wanted to grow. So, my next move was to become a manager of the restaurant. I did this for many years and eventually trained to be a chef and even the general manager of the restaurant. I was able to serve over 1.7 Million people in fourteen years, and I even found my wife at this restaurant. This was an outstanding training ground for service.

The recipe for success, no matter what one is trying to serve, starts with great ingredients and love. After collecting these ingredients, it is vital to follow the recipe and avoid shortcuts. There is more about this part in each of our minds, including mine. I learned that whenever a shortcut to success or money is employed, the likelihood of lasting success can be derailed. The way that I hadn't failed was always through service. We increased our sales through service. We became the poster children for how excellent & caring service boosted the top-line sales of the restaurant. We all got on the same page and worked to love our guests. If nothing else, display we care for the guests, as though they are guests in our own homes, in our own lives. If something didn't go right that day for the guest, we were all empowered to make it right. We didn't want the server or bartender to have to ask us questions about whether it was OK to buy dinner or an appetizer for someone if things didn't go well. We managed the restaurant from a position of release, not control. We allowed the entire team to choose how to treat the guests, that is, in the same manner they would want to be treated.

Even this "treat them as you would want to be treated" didn't work for some of the service team. The problem was that some of them had never been treated very well. We had to identify when this was the case, one employee at a time, and work with them to ensure they understood they were worthy of receiving excellent service and worthy of giving outstanding service. Releasing the team to achieve the best inside themselves, thus giving the same to the guests, was the secret sauce to our success. Caring and allowing others to care was the secret ingredient to service, and preparing excellent food for others to enjoy was the rest.

This concept, give and let give, is addictive. It is vital to our successes, no matter where we seek them. So, if it is a Master of Sales degree you intend to achieve in the future, you must first master giving. Exceed the expectations of those around you. Care about how others feel. Make others know that their story, their life, and their life force are essential to you. Help those you serve (& sell to) feel loved. Above all, I love them.

What would Grandma do? Please give them a cool drink. Serve them some farm-fresh ingredients of your own. If that means giving them integrity and a loving ear, then do that. If that means caring more for your customer than you care for making a sale, then do that. If that means being authentic, like the ingredients you love the most, then do that. And if that means treating them better than you may have been treated, or like you wish you would have been treated, or like you know you want to be treated, then do that. Do for those you serve what makes you feel good about when the same thing is done for you. Be the salesman you wish you could find every time you need to buy something. You can do amazing things if you put your mind to it.

Find the ingredients, those you wish to serve to others, that you want to be part of the recipe of your life. Then hone them, practice using these ingredients, and serve up some tasty experiences for your clients! I'm getting hungry. Maybe a roasted chicken with roasted potatoes and cauliflower, baked with onion, carrot, and celery sprinkled with orange zest and drizzled with balsamic, would be excellent for dinner. Maybe I will invite someone over and serve them something that makes them feel good.

If you serve it, they will come.

Exercise:

Choose the ingredients you decide to serve others wisely. Pretend you are the perfect dish, and write down the ingredients (words) you want to be used when people describe you. This is a fun exercise. Even name yourself as a dish if you wish. Here's an idea to run with...

Healthy, Smiling & Fun Quiche

Two parts listener

1 part conversationist

1 part curious

1 part smile

1 part growth

1 part worldly

1 part helper

1 part educator

1 part kindness

1 part giver

1 part forgiver

Mix these freshly picked ingredients on a daily basis, and blend them in a stainless bucket. Ask a friend to help you prep and uniquely cook them all, and then serve warm. It is excellent when served with coffee or tea. Serves 3-4 people. Increase amounts accordingly, the more significant the group.

There's nothing more fun than making and serving a fresh "you" each day. Very satisfying.

Chapter 7

Cost of Ingredients

Know your business...

Focusing on the top line (sales) is only part of a good business plan. The other parts are sometimes more challenging to master. From the largest country to the most petite person within that country, each entity must know the cost of the ingredients to keep the business of life flowing smoothly.

"Let's get down to business; I don't get no time to play around; what is this? Must be a circus in town; let's shut the shit down on these clowns; can I get a witness (hell yeah!)." If you've never heard this song, maybe a foray into Eminem would do your mind right.

I can't say it was brilliant to let my four-year-old kids learn every Eminem song when I was deep in the throes of fourteen years building homes, but it did pump me up, and believe it or not, they loved the songs and still do. We sang out loud together, even when Monica Lewinsky was reduced to a simple lyric in a song; they didn't know what I knew. Find that one if you haven't; you'll see what I mean. Now, bear with me. It doesn't mean they knew what the lyrics meant, and sometimes, we are all just four-year-olds running our businesses. Throwing them into the reality of life was my technique for getting them to see life is filled with all sorts of lyrics.

I didn't ever go to school to become a businessman, and maybe I should have. But the school of life is sometimes more real. I surrounded myself with lyrics and art in my spare time and wanted to learn more about other cultures. I traveled alone in Europe for three months in 1987, was able to see the Berlin wall when it was still there, and dove off sixty-foot cliffs into the Santorini Mediterranean. I was thirsty to experience life, and I did just that.

My mentor in business was a Harvard Business School-educated man. He ran restaurants like a business that isn't supposed to fail but instead is supposed to be there for the children to run someday and for the whole community to enjoy for decades to come. He knows who he is, and he is fantastic.

As an owner, he taught me the value of understanding one's costs when running a business. He believed sales would fix nearly every-thing unless you forgot to focus on costs. So it's a dance. Spare no expense to build sales, but don't spend too much doing it. That one took a while to wrap my head around.

Years later, I tried my hand at business with his mindset. I started a building company in 2005 and did a thorough job of becoming a thriving business within just a year or two. Then, in 2008, things got real. Seventy-five percent of the homebuilders failed during this economic challenge, yet my business didn't. But it did cost me the home I had just built for my family to get out of the quicksand of the situation I found myself in. What I learned through that era is that when one has their home in the same business as their busi-ness (real estate), if the economy fails and the value of real estate falls nearly in half, it can be almost impossible to keep the business rolling.

It wasn't impossible. I kept it going. People talk about blood, sweat, and tears. Yeah, I have experienced all of these. Adversity was upon the family, me, and all of my clients. Yet, somehow, we all got through. I helped my clients surf the situation by pushing costs lower and squeezing dozens of percent off their build. It was a time for all of us to survive. The banks squeezed everyone because even their business plans were failing. They thought they knew and understood their business plans, but many banks failed.

When banks fail, we all fail. It is hard to stop there.

Back to Eminem. "Must be a circus in town; let's shut the shit down on these clowns; can I get a witness (hell yeah!)."

However, as I worked to stay positive and leave the blame on the back burner, I pushed the business forward for many years to follow. When my wife had the double mastectomy and chemotherapy some years later, it also hit me and the kids like a ton of bricks. I had been so focused on keeping costs down for my homeowners and myself that the only way to keep the business going was by adding volume. This works with cookies. But it doesn't really work the same with custom homes.

Slowly, I had no time for my family, which needed me to be *present* more than ever. I had too many homeowners to focus on each of them. And I was selling the cookies that cost me $2.00 each to make for $1.75. This meant that every time I sold a cookie, I was going deeper into debt.

How did I forget the concept of focusing on sales and costs at the same time? Time was the problem. I starved myself of time. Time is money. And while money isn't everything, the lack of it is nothing. And this is how it all fails.

Please don't make the same mistake that I made. Please focus on the cost of your ingredients (your budget.)

Another way to look at this is through the prism of sports. There are two types of professional sports heroes. Some make it to the Bigs and, push their bodies toward a cliff, and then jump. Some decide to buy a parachute early in their careers. These sportspeople choose to think ahead. What will be next after sports?

What you buy while you are in business is just as crucial to your future as what you sell and how you serve. Those who use and invest their money wisely are able to be there to serve and teach others long-term.

There will be many downturns in our lives. If we focus on how to retain the funds we earn, we will enable ourselves to withstand the curve balls that get thrown our way.

The Harvard Business School mindset can be distilled in one introductory sentence (probably should be three sentences, or a paragraph, or a ton of tuition, but oh well.) <u>There are many costs to making others feel good about your business, so focus on both *Sales and Costs* in order to enable yourselves to sell (& serve) more while being there for others for the long run, and thus, allowing yourselves to pass the test of time (the most limited resource that exists in a lifetime.)</u>

Look at your clients and see them as who they have been for a lifetime up to now. Talk to them by getting them to talk about themselves. Smile at them, acknowledging that they make you feel good. Thank them once you have helped serve them.

If you haven't failed before, you may not have tried enough yet. Failure is critical to learning. Education helps a ton, too. I chose to learn outside of traditional knowledge and college. It is doable, yet a nice blend of both is a great way to proceed.

Listen to Eminem. Realize that some start with nothing and rise to be a star. Realize that being true to oneself, one's mindset and one's journey are valuable. This is called the school of hard knocks in some circles. I call it your recipe for success. Everything you choose to do is part of the recipe. Choices are equivalent to learning. All your experiences are part of how you can serve others in whatever field you choose. Choose wisely, but choose. Don't get stuck on the cliff with no parachute. And realize that a college degree is just as valuable as being talented at a sport. Life lessons are gained when we try and fail. Probably you will be excellent at something. What are you exceptional at? Please write it down. Then, it would be best if you pursued how to serve others in the field where you show aptitude and talent.

The value placed on any one thing, person, or idea won't make a life or dish great. It is all the ingredients and the lessons we learn about how to pay attention to the cost of the ingredients and how we choose to blend them that lead to our unique recipe for life.

Some have a taste for money in how they choose their success, sometimes at a cost to other parts of their lives. Others blend in a bit more service to others in their pursuit, also at a price. If it could be taught early, and people were capable of learning from others instead of making their own mistakes, then life would be much simpler. No matter how many classes there are to learn lessons, I sense there is no college large enough to teach us everything. And that would cost hella money anyway. We all have our taste for what success means to us.

The anatomy of service is probably every bit as complicated as the anatomy of your own body. Why does it work? What parts aren't working so well? How should we work on the parts that have their challenges? How do we remodel ourselves?

Keep pushing to learn about yourself. Do this in your spare time. Then, go out and learn about others and what you can do for them. You will be surprised at how interconnected the process of serving others is to serving yourself. These two concepts require the best ingredients. Love, a positive mindset, a giving spirit, and all the other great ingredients you can muster.

When we find ourselves using unhealthy ingredients in any part of our process, then we have more work to do.

Hubris is dangerous. Overconfidence has crept into my life in the past. The setbacks learned from this hubris are the guardrails of my life. Do you have too much pride or not enough? Either way, we have a responsibility to all those around us to keep both overconfidence and timidness as guardrails. Choose something. But take some time to think about what you choose. Stay within the guardrails on the road of life.

When service to others is the choice, we most often start to feel better right off the bat. Service is my addiction. In the field of sales I have chosen, I want to serve others I work with, and I want to serve my clients. All of this results in service to myself. But thinking "I'm all that" is not where I have decided to go because it compromises one's integrity to do so. I have decided to plumb the depths of my mind to find a healthier mindset. This has allowed me to feel way less judgmental about others. Who am I to be better than anyone else? I am nobody and everybody at the same time.

It was when I realized this that I started to become more effective. The prejudices we carry with us are either a bitter ingredient that makes our dish both lose flavor and cost us way too much or a weight we carry with us, ultimately holding us back from tremendous success. How will someone unlike us or who we don't totally understand want to eat what we are serving them if we don't do it with love? Seek to understand these people. They will then better understand you when this is your strategy for service (& sales.)

Love is the ingredient that costs nothing and adds the most to every recipe.

And if you haven't listened to enough Eminem, get one of his albums and let yourself go. He is different than you, and at the same time, he is just like you. He wants to be loved—time to grow your mindset.

Chapter 8

Price and Marketing

Be Memorable, Be You, Become Your Culture

The culture of a service organization is critical to increasing sales. Companies can either decide to be the best service at the best price, the best service at an affordable price, or excellent quality for the price, etc. If you want to be with a great company, make a great decision on which company you choose to join.

Every industry has its leaders. How do you decide to be part of the right team? If you want to be chosen to be on a team, then be very clear about what you are looking for in a team from day one. While you may have learned that you are being interviewed for a position, there is a way to present the concept that you are interviewing companies for the right fit. This will ensure you set the right tone for making the best choice from the beginning and will dramatically increase the chances that you end up being part of a great culture.

When I decided to leave the home building industry, it was vital for me to find a new industry where I could thrive and, at the same time, spend a ton of time with my family. After all, the main reason that construction ended up being the wrong fit for me was how volatile the real estate market could be. If I were to work over sixty to seventy hours per week, then I would not end up having enough time for my family. After the health crisis my wife faced, I learned that there was no reason for me to spend so many hours away from her and the kids. And in fact, if I choose to do so, I may end up losing them altogether.

Before the building, the restaurant industry faced the same challenges. All weekends and evenings away from the family which left me yearning for something that allowed me more time with the family. No matter which direction I turned, service to others was proving to be a challenge that stressed me to the limits. Whether being stretched across several counties with building projects or being stretched across the face of a clock that wouldn't allow me to watch my kids grow up, I knew that my next move would have to allow me to change my mindset.

I wanted to serve others; that was a given. But by doing so, I learned that it had to be good for my family and me in order to provide me with the strength that it takes to be available to those I serve. No matter what, please don't allow yourself to give less to your family than you do your clients. So, how does it look to achieve this?

Equipoise - What? Kind of like it sounds. Let's dive in a bit and find a way for you to achieve personal equilibrium or equipoise. We are working to find the manner in which opposing life forces can be equal. When equipoise enters our life, we feel it. It can be significant. Do you love what you do? If not, then find something else to do. Does the thing you love to do make you want to learn more about it? If not, then change what you do. But if you were to answer yes to either of those questions and know what it feels like to have a position at a company that allows you to find your equipment, then you have found the beginnings of the best path for yourself.

So when you're interviewing companies to work with, have many questions for them about what drives them at this company and what the interviewer loves about the company. Ask how they ended up with this company. Ask what about the culture is ultra-satisfying and what about the culture could get better. Ask what this interviewer is doing to try to make the culture better. And ask what the company has done in the past year to make the culture better. This is a place that will either match your family life needs or will not. They will either see your family as important to them or they will not. This company will either get it, or they won't.

If the company is working to serve you, then you will be able to serve their guests or clients. There is no better way to approach this work-personal relationship than this. Remember, the opposing forces are work life and home life. And if they place your family before their bottom line, then they get it. And in the end, you can rest assured they will put the needs of their clients before their own as well.

Yes, all companies are in it for the money. But if they don't understand that their company is nothing more than a series of families collaborating to serve a bunch of clients' families, then thank them for their time and look for a different place to be.

Does the company you work with believe in paying on a timely basis? If cash flow gets tight, will they take care of their own needs before they take care of your family's needs? These are hard questions for companies to answer. But if this company you are choosing to work with is in line with your service mindset, then you will be able to achieve unbelievable results with them. If they see themselves as the most essential part of their company, then they won't be able to make it under the limbo bar of success. The limbo dance is complex and takes excellent flexibility. A company should be able to limbo better than you, and you should be able to learn from them.

On the same subject, make sure they can learn from you. Your ability to serve needs to set an example for your company. If you show them how to "get stuff done" and not complain while doing it, you are more likely to change their culture for the better than most. Become the culture you want to be part of, but make sure they already know how to be there for you before you even start working with the company you are interviewing.

Price – How much are you worth? If you want to be worth more than others in the company, then prove it. If you want your clients to receive an excellent value for the money they pay, then become the great value you seek for them. When I am selling, I try to avoid the concept of price. "We can give you a better price than the competition." So, where are the shortcuts the competition is taking? Which people are they exploiting along the way? How can they give such a reasonable price when it is difficult for us to provide the great value we offer at the fair price we are charging?

Hidden costs of goods sold and labor shortcuts are a sure sign that a company is willing to take advantage of you.

Have you ever explained to a client the concept of warranty and how important it is for a company to still be there for you years or even decades later? This is an excellent time to peruse the concept of inflation. Let's say that a company is willing to sell you Solar Panels at the best price, which is a number that the competition can't seem to meet in order to be awarded the job. Both your company and the other cheaper company were able to provide twenty-five-year materials and labor warranty. You know your product is superior to theirs, so that explains why it should cost a little more. But still, they come in 15-20% cheaper than your bid. How can that be?

Here are a few forgotten factors that the company is sweeping under the carpet. (a) If they have to come back in 10 years to warrant the system, the service call price will likely double due to inflation during those 10 years. So, if the service call had been $500 this year, then the exact cost of the call would likely have been $1000 ten years later. (b) The materials they are quoting with the system will likely be out of date by 10 years later, and it will cost a premium to get them. Let's say another $2000. However, if they had bought your superior product for $2000 more and not had the warranty issue in the first place, it would have saved a lot of headaches in the first place. Then, (c) the company that had more warranty issues over the 10 years most likely had to go out of business because they had undercharged for inflation and used the inferior product to make sure they got the sale.

The companies that think long-term ensure they offer a reasonable price, but typically not the best price. Often, these companies understand the power of having no issues over time. That means no problems with their product and no issues with their team. They treat the team well, they treat the customer respectfully by supplying the best product available, and they have a superior word of mouth about the quality they offer. In the end, the clients say great things about their product, and the people who serve them will be worth talking about to their friends. Great reviews happen when we all focus on the right things and give the best service and quality products to our clients.

This Increases Production Worldwide Today! Another example is in the world of Solar, to stay on topic. If two companies were competing for your business and each had a different plan for a successful array for your home (so you would have two other choices), which would you instead choose: (1) Let's say Company A suggested 30 solar panels make all your power for a year. But to keep them running optimally, they should always be clean as when they were new. To complicate things, the cleaning must occur whenever they are soiled and while they are cool (at night) to keep the warranty intact. So pollen, dust storms, bird poop, leaves, and the sun itself make this virtually impossible. However, suppose the Company A sales representative kind of sweeps the point of maintenance under the sales rug and sidesteps direct questions about maintenance. In that case, he is typically able to avoid answering the question and ensure the immediate sale at hand goes through (we assume over 85% of Solar Companies do this sales pitch...). Or (2) Company B gives you an alternative, that is, Company B suggests doing at least 10% fewer panels (27) because they offer an automated solar panel cleaning system that will ensure the production of the system runs 15-30% better on an annual basis and will degrade over ten years at 1-1.5% instead of the Company A degradation rate of 5% over ten years. This means that Company B's choice will make the panels degrade over three times slower, thus lasting much longer and producing more power annually than Company A. And finally, *Company B offers their system at the same price!* With the automated system, just set it and forget it, and reduce the risk of some future panel cleaner falling to an injury or death while always getting the most production possible.

When I ask this question to a buyer, nearly 100% of them choose the Company B idea and decide to move forward. Question: Why would company A keep doing it the old way, which is worse for the homeowner? This is one of the most vexing questions in all of 2024 green energy sales. The simple answer is complicated. But below are a few of the outdated thought processes that Company A likes to respond with to keep from having to upset their own Solar Cart (apples are so much easier to sell!) See below. What are your thoughts here (mine in parentheses)? Imagine you own the Solar Company.

- Introducing a new sales idea to the sales team is too hard. (Give your team some credit for how smart they are! Better yet, give your clients the truth so you will survive as a company!!)
- Avoiding the hard questions makes the sale go forward easier. (So, does Company A believe an easy sale is better than an honest sale? Most all the Solar companies are saying yes to this one...Why?) Again, failure always follows this mindset. I have been there.
- New technology isn't proven (not correct; instead, this cleaning system has been proven for 14 years already, in 14 countries, on millions of panels daily.)
- More moving parts are more complex to manage. (Tell that to Amazon or Walmart or Home Depot.)
- Where are the white papers and case studies (over 600 of them exist, yet Company A refuses to read them; why? Who knows, really...)

Lessons: As a customer, demand the best and truth. As a team member, demand the best for your customers and truth. As a company, please do your best for both and tell the truth! If this is too hard for you, then choose a more straightforward business model that fits your mindset. You are capable of great things... all of you. Do great things. And please, do the right thing.

Marketing – The best marketing plan is achieved through (*a*) *having a purpose*. When companies know why they do what they do, the customer wins. When the people who work at a company know why they work at a company and align their own "why" with the company's "why," then the customer wins again. Next, (*b*) *testi-*

monials drive sales. When the clients love the company, they tell others. When the team that runs a company loves the company, then there are satisfied team members serving satisfied clients—satisfaction stew baby. You've heard of "happy-go-lucky," and when everyone is happy, we are all lucky. We need a bit of luck to do a good job. Happiness drives luck. (c) *Search Engine Optimization (SEO) is easy when everyone loves your service and product.* Then hire a happy marketing team, and make sure they understand how sales are driven by happiness (remember the Satisfaction vs Frustration exercise? Revisit it.)

KISS Method – Keep the sales team happy, and hire happy salespeople, and everyone will be satisfied. It seems too easy. (Don't forget about operations too! Another book.) It is easy, but living it day to day is even easier when one person at a time is on board with the idea and is in love with service. Try it. (d) Explore new mediums. Too many companies are afraid of change because they are already experiencing some sales growth. But what if sales growth could be explosive? Ask the team what we could do better, then, for heaven's sake, listen. And try some of what they are saying, seriously. I have a story about this and how companies would instead not tell their customers about maintenance for their product in order to not focus on a potential reason not to buy... Dumb. Oh yeah, I just told this story above, and it is still a more profound story for another time. *Include a cause or a purpose in your value proposition.* I mentioned earlier how value propositions are too often just words. The added value needs to be accurate and feel great. Sacrifice a little profit and make what you do more valuable. Profit is exciting; we all know this. But adding value is way more exciting. It will drive sales year after year, and this will drive the long-term success you seek. Don't just have a proposition; be a *preposition* when it comes to sales.

Prepositions – We look *within* ourselves and see *beyond* now and *toward* the future; we dig *inside* to try harder, and then we run *through* the finish line to lift ourselves. Lift others. (Love lifts us where we belong.) It's another song, but darn it, they work. We take you *with* us on our journey, and we know that this plus and that minus are the synergy that helps us all achieve our needs. Simple math here, people. Value prepositions bring us *past* the past and help us *under* the limbo bar. They rock. The prepositions are Queen singing, "We will, we will rock you!" OK, maybe that's a stretch, but Damn, I love Queen—value prepositions, not value propositions. Let's Go!

Be You! Remember, nobody else can be you. You are super-unique and bring everything needed to the table. Set the table and serve a tasty and memorable meal. Go out on a limb (without a saw) and give fantastic service (& sales.) Then, watch everyone marvel at how you do it. This is the most fun part of your life. How about not only being you but being better than you? This is the part I am working diligently on each day. It's tough, 'nuff said. But it is so much more fun than the alternative and the old way of thinking.

Chapter 9

The Chameleon

Remember this Chapter!!!

Chameleons are fascinating. Cindy Lauper, *True Colors* jumps to the front of my mind whenever I hear the word or see one of these little reptiles. What if we could change our True Colors?

At this time in history, where the colors of the rainbow (and nature, for that matter) scare a portion of the population because it reminds some people that anyone different than ourselves should be "othered" or may strike a *woke* nerve in various political circles, we have seen colors themselves take on their own political lives. There are the rainbows, the black lives people, white supremacy people, green enthusiasts, and red scares (and you name it) to worry about in our everyday discourse.

So we have taken the one thing we love to do, which is to connect, and instead have made it more difficult to achieve. Colors have certainly played their parts in the story. Division is at an all-time high from what I see in the day-to-day marketplace and world. So why does it seem many are trying to divide us and tear us apart from living and loving in a harmonious world? This, too, is probably another book altogether. Maybe the people who are making the rules in the marketplace are experimenting with how to keep us all "othering" each other, so in the end, *we, the people,* lack the collective resolve to move things when they need to be moved. We can solve these problems, have extreme hope, and be a part of solutions. Obvious things should be changed when they need to be changed when things that aren't right just aren't right. But there seems to be a force that holds us back from doing so. Something is stopping us from making change easier. We likely need a little more *"chameleonatomy"* (new word alert...but it works for me. Hear me out.) With chameleonatomy, we shall overcome even today's most challenging issues.

The tendency for one group to want to demonize another has never been more front and center than it is right now. At the same time, the "wedge fatigue" (when people try to drive a wedge between various groups) we all feel is indeed wearing us all down. I'm tired of being tired of it. I'm ready to help change it. One person, one discussion, one idea at a time, we can do it.

I was able to meet Barack Obama on his campaign before he was president. Now, I'm not saying I'm solely a Democrat (Regan was great, too,) but this is just a story and guy that struck a chord with me. In his campaign, he talked about how one voice can make a huge change. It is true. I do wish the message of one voice would gain steam again. The reason for keeping the dialogue going is precisely to solve the "wedge fatigue" problem. When Obama told me that he needed my help, his one device to my one voice, I heard it. I helped with the campaign in various ways from that point forward (another story). My wife had been making phone calls for him at a rate nearly unparalleled by other callers. She was fired up. Her enthusiasm was contagious for me to witness, so I joined in, and we were all working on something together that would help us be a part of the change we sought.

I was wanting to follow anyone who appeared to be a good leader toward the vision of an America greater than myself. I was hoping America could be based less on selfishness and more on selflessness. I wanted to be a better version of myself than I had displayed up to this time. I was hoping to change. I wanted America to be there, better and more robust, for my children. So, if the other guy vying for the job had shaken my hand and appealed to my inner desire to be part of something great, I can't say I wouldn't have considered giving him my vote. The key is that we need good leaders in order to create a good product in the world. Vote for the leader you want our kids to be like someday. Vote for the leader that inspires you. Vote for the leader whom you would let watch your kids for a month if you had to go on a special secret mission (well, I doubt that will happen, but you get it...). Vote.

As business owners and service teams, none of us are indeed any different than a president, a single mom or dad, a teacher, or a wounded warrior. We all want the best for those we serve, or else we won't have a product (often the product is ourselves or our country) that sells in the world for very long. Let's not marginalize ourselves; instead, we should be amazing people. Let's give memorable service to each other.

And the truth is, we instinctively "want to all just get along." But the perception is, "We can't just all get along." There's that word. Can't. No good, we *can do* better. We teach our kids about a "can do" mentality. And darn it, we can do it. "I can't jump this high," I remember standing at the high jump bar in seventh grade, thinking this. By eighth grade, I had already learned to say it a different way. I can jump higher. This is the year I won the CYO City Championship while Mt. Saint Helens was blowing up behind the grand-stands. Sometimes, you have to blow and do something incredible.

We need to be more empathetic, and feel each other's pain, and respect each other's histories, families, and sense of self. Chameleonatomy (now added to my auto-correct dictionary on my computer) could be defined as 1. *One's adaptive ability to see, feel, sense, and display the need for loving one's neighbor for 360 degrees of direction toward and beyond all those with which we know and serve. 2. The study of the structure, interconnection, or internal workings of something.*

The second definition, about our interconnection with one another and the relationship of our moods and mindset to those we communicate with, is the part that really fascinates me. When we are sharing information, educating, listening to and serving others and generally in the same "head-space," we are more likely to be open to learning, able to see the future more clearly, and probably more susceptible to learning how something outside of us could be good or better for us. Look closely at this paragraph. I was tempted to write this in all caps, but then I would have made it seem likely I was yelling this question... (Maybe my gut tells me to cry them, but I am going to write them instead calmly.) *Are we more likely to get in the same mindset as someone if we seek to understand theirs as much as possible before we start getting them to hear our proposal?* Italics work almost as well.

The concept of Chameleonatomy is catching once one opens his mind to it. How connected we are, almost like quantum physics, is deserving of more excellent study. It is maybe even contagious. There are many facets of the concept to unearth, but it may take another entire book (or library) to develop the study of this field fully. After all, how long did it take for the study of Anatomy to unfold?

Relating the properties inherent to chameleons is only part of this concept. Isn't it possible that all animals and plants share similar traits? We can all imagine what it would be like to walk a mile in another man's shoes. But we don't really get a chance to do it. What if we could walk a year in another man's skin? What if we could feel the mood that others have and why they feel it? What if, in addition to changing sexes, we could all change races for a while or even become more like other animals? If we think like a chameleon, we are more likely to listen to others, empathize with others, and understand others. Horses do this. Dogs do this. PETA would love this. Cruelty to other beings would be drastically reduced.

Chameleon physiology allows them to physically display the idea I am explaining through the color of their skin changes to match their mood and surroundings. Part of why it works for them is to blend in with the background, and the other part is so the other chameleons know what their mood is. And in some ways, our physiology does the same. We blush when embarrassed, we get in a good mood when others are in a good mood, we yawn when others yawn, and we even often want to fade into the background if a situation seems dangerous. Sympathetic nervous systems are both complicated and critical to the process of understanding and relating to others. Thus, it is essential in the process of serving (& sales.)

Chameleonatomy is a force within us all that also allows us to serve each other better. It brings us satisfaction to serve and help others. When we are around a big group of people, at a dinner party, for instance, and somebody starts to clear dishes, what do we do? We all pitch in and want to help. We pitch in if our chameleonatomy is feeling it. But sometimes, we don't feel like pitching in. Then what?

The Inner Chameleon – So you don't feel like serving? How do we solve this one? And how does it help us serve one another better by actually solving this feeling? Just serve, regardless of how much you feel like serving. You've probably already noticed this, and if not, try it sometime. Somehow, helping others and serving makes us feel better. It's just in our nature to help and serve. Like the mom wanting to serve the baby in the opening chapter, it is in our DNA to do so. It strikes me that the metaphor for how to overcome all the biases we see and hear around us is to become more closely in tune with our *inner chameleon*.

If we don't feel like pitching in, we are less in tune with our *inner chameleon* right then. Change the channel, and tune into the *inner chameleon* channel. It's like watching Natural Geographic. Soothing, calm, and thus serve us what we need. It nurses us and nourishes us. Become the chameleon and feel better through service to others.

Years ago, my brother told me one night when we were coming home from a dance club that he thought I was basically a chameleon. "You don't really have your personality; you have everyone else's personality that you are talking with or hanging around." For a few minutes, the comment took me aback. Now, this can be a bit dangerous if you're hanging with the wrong crowd, and it is, in fact, why we don't want our kids to hang with the wrong crowd. I have grappled for years with his comment, yet it started to seem more and more accurate the further I dug into the service (& sales) industry. Suppose I exercise situational awareness of the people around me and their need to be seen, noticed and understood. In that case, I am tapping into the service mindset and becoming the chameleon. Chamelonatomy may be a course of study for our future service and sales educators to develop further. How could you help make strides in this field? Be a pioneer. Serve. Follow a healthy path to sales...Love-love service (tennis, anyone??)

Don't be afraid to let them go... Your true colors. They're beautiful...

And another thing... ah, never mind. Serve for a while before reading more.

Chapter 10

You Had Me at Hello

What makes you feel good when you first see someone?

For me, it is watching them smile at me and seeing their eyes wrinkle at the corners. I mean, *Really Seeing Their Eyes!* So, when we are in sales and planning to serve someone, how do we go about making this happen?

Some of you may be asking yourself, how does one increase the chances of a smile from the person that either just opened the front door, came onto the car lot, stepped into the doctor's office, or has been teaching my daughter at school? This doesn't feel natural to everyone because many people haven't been taught this, and many have certainly never gone forward as life progressed to learn this action. I'm lucky; I had a Mom who innately knew how to do this. She knew how to make her face blossom like a flower. Some are naturally magnetic humans, and others aren't.

If you work for someone else, or if you work for yourself, you may have noticed that there are some people each day who you naturally seem to get along with and others that seem to make you feel awkward automatically or want to cringe.

In Character vs The Character – Now, imagine being in a play and walking on stage. We've all seen a performance where there is a character that just kills their part from the instant he (or she or they) walks onto the scene. This is known as *being in character*. This person pulls us into his character's mindset naturally and viscerally. If the character is trying to be a curmudgeon and make sure that others around him will avoid him at all costs, this one channels his (or her) *inner grump*.

To visualize this, imagine coming face-to-face with a Wolverine. These animals don't make good pets, which means they can be aggressive because they are unpredictable and dangerous when angry or upset. They tend just to want to kill things and eat them. So that isn't generally what the human version of the Wolverine does, but hear me out once again...

I've never seen someone walking his wolverine (but some dogs I've met sure have seemed like they wanted to be the grumpy animal.) The curmudgeon would rather stay in their natural habitat, and if they stray out into the world to buy more groceries or get the mail, maybe steer clear of them. We can all likely visualize one or two of these types in our own lives. Or maybe there is a second idea to try... give it a try sometime to see how it works. It doesn't hurt to give this one a shot, experiment a little in your communication journey, and do something that, to some, has become a little counterintuitive (in today's world...). Try a *Smile*. Don't stop trying.

Door-to-door sales are not easy, but once learned, it is an enriching way to spend one's work day. However, some of the downsides are the dogs, and sometimes the people, and occasionally the weather. No wonder some people get paid like doctors to do this job. It is work.

Imagine walking up to someone's house when their dog is aggressively trying to make sure you know that it absolutely hates you and wants you gone now! I have often asked myself, "Now, why does the person like to allow the dog to act this way?" Being a bit of a student of animals, I've come up with a few ideas to explain this phenomenon. What is interesting is that many dog owners blame it on the dog... Really? Don't tell Caesar that! No self-respecting dog whisperer will allow the dog to keep acting this way if they want other people to casually come to their home and enjoy cookies and milk or a glass of wine or bring the neighbor kids over to play hoops. If I see a trampoline, I want to jump on it later with the kids. This is how my mind overcomes things; I set *micro-goals* at the moment and try to achieve them. And I want to be like Caesar and control the dog's mind, getting it to succumb to its inner cat and just purr by the end of this experience.

Being grumpy is a talent that many will use as a defense mechanism to ensure that you feel like giving up and leaving them alone. The grumps teach it to their dogs just the same. I like to try to un-teach it.

Curmudgeon is the word I don't take lightly when serving others, but I still want to serve them just the same. I have known and served several of them, and it is often true that they have become this way over time. However, the more time I spend with them and learn more about their past, the more excellent their dog acts toward me. ***Make sense?*** (Always use this question when selling. It is like putting a pin in it so you can move forward to the next concept.)

Remember, it is the ADVERSITY that we seek when we are providing service. It is *the adversity* that provides us with our superpowers to help the people who come next, those who really need our help.

If one's nature is to drive others away (dogs and humans do this) to avoid discussion and confrontation, then it is wise first to ask yourself if you really want to have this conversation at all. Mostly, the people you are serving need help with many parts of their lives. Overcome the adversity you witness, and keep the conversations going forward.

So what softens them up if they have lacked the love through their life to allow them to keep their softened spirit more malleable? Answer just below, but quick observation here first...

The 'watchdog' type people in the world are just a little scared and are (like the dog) likely worried someone is going to take advantage of them or their property, so they are ready for it all moments and will be a difficult person to soften slightly. This is where the superhero side of you steps forward. And they do soften. But others are softer on the inside, over 99% of the time. Just like with the dog softening, it can take quite a bit of time and sometimes takes no time at all.

I have witnessed this every day in the field. Again, most of the more complex people soften up, usually quite quickly. And as far as the actual dogs go, in four years and tens of thousands of homes I've visited door-to-door, and by walking right up to and past (without even acknowledging their tactics often) every barking dog as though I know them, *I have been bitten only once.* A pit bull to boot. That was just because there were four dogs, and they competed with each other while they were addressing the new person coming into their domain, just like the people that lived at the dog owners' home where I was a bit.

My dad was a veterinarian, so we learned early to have no fear and focus on the people who love the dog. If the person becomes nice, the dog will too. The dog had hit a vein, and I had to apply direct pressure and leave for the gas station to buy first aid immediately and get it cleaned up, but the blood on the driveway was memorable for all involved. *Observation:* If people stay mean and escalate, will the dog do the same? Yep. It sure seems that way. And dogs do like it when you talk to them in a low and goofy voice. Their owners say things this way to them, so go ahead and do the same—familiarity breeds. Learn the dog's (and human's) name and use it.

Ok, back to the question above, what is the answer?

Smile. (*And let them see you doing it in a way that makes you genuinely glad they are there!*) *Let a smile wash over your face, and decide that you're going to love this person, no matter what.*

A growing smile on your face for the first seconds you make contact with a person is scientifically proven to soften the other person's demeanor. Forbes Magazine had an article published on April 13, 2020, stating that *New Study Shows Forming A Simple Smile Tricks Your Mind Into A Positive Mood* (*by Bryan Robinson, Ph.D.*)

The main idea is based on a new study published in *Experimental Psychology* that reports "the sheer activity of moving your facial muscles to form a smile – even if you fake it – generates positive emotions and raises your mood."

Here's how it works in essence: One acts like they are happy to see another and is in a good mood, and *your pretend becomes the reality.* And then, through repetition, your reality becomes increasingly positive. Malcolm Gladwell would likely say to do this over 10,000 times to become an expert at it.

When we watch this unfold on the stage, we know it is true. When the characters make us laugh or are jovial toward one another, we actually laugh and release positive endorphins. Which means drum roll here.... **The person you are serving is your**

audience! How hard was that? Not hard at all. We've seen it in movies, on Broadway, or at our kid's Christmas school play. The energy brought by those on the stage and in the audience is at odds with each other in the first seconds, but as the moments go by, the actors bring us along for the story. *We are actors, people, and the audience (other people).*

Goal: ***Be the reason someone smiles.*** *Do this all day long; rinse and repeat.*

Today, we may be sore, sick, or generally depressed, but if we jump on the stage for the performance with a new mindset, we will then become endearing to the audience and get an excellent review of the play. We may even help someone with the badger-like day they were experiencing and help them change their faith in human nature itself by the end of the experience. People are changed by each other. People who learn how to serve one another especially are capable of helping to change other people and must do so.

When we are in sales, we are the helpers - Change is the goal with whatever product we are representing. We want to help make the other person have a better chance at being satisfied with the life they were born into and maybe be changed by their experience and our product. If saving money is giving a better life, then hopefully, we represent a product that does just this. If making the world a better place helps customers see the world in a slightly less harsh prism, then let's do it. Let's seek out everyone, not just the easy ones. Let's help those who find it hard to help themselves. Again, the first step is to ***grow a smile and twinkle in your eye from the very moment you meet someone***, and then blossom into seeing this person (and ourselves) as someone deserving of love and our most positive energies.

Imagine that while you are knocking on a door, the person opening it is someone you love. Then the door opens, and you then find yourself saying, "I love you (Dad, or Grandma, or Sister), and I really miss you; how have you been?" You aren't really saying *these words,* but **think of them** while you are improvising your natural greeting for this person. Each greeting should be specific to the person you are meeting because this person is unique in the world. *Most importantly, remember again, they are a person in the world.* They were born. They were a child that people loved, breastfed (maybe), changed their diapers (hopefully), and helped to walk (most likely.) This person, this bright young woman or man, and even this badger or curmudgeon across from you were once this child that had to grow and learn how to communicate with people. Some had a good step up on their competition because they were guided and stewarded through their young life, while others were abused, forgotten, left to fend for themselves, and lonely (maybe these latter become the curmudgeons?)

What's In An Eye? – The eye of a person generally looks the same from the time they were born to the time they stop serving (die...). When I was young, I had allergies, and when I would rub my eye, my dad would say, "You have something in your eye?" Then, while nodding my head yes, he would say, "It's your finger." I always loved that one, but maybe it wasn't the most empathetic of responses he could have mustered. The main thing he was trying to teach me was to be (a) more challenging and innovative and (b) wash your face instead of scratching at the eye. It's always good to take care of your eyes, as the lack of them is undoubtedly more challenging to endure. My blind dog and half-blind brother would both attest to this. In fact, 3 years ago, I contracted double vision when I caught Valley Fever. Now medicated, it is solved, but I did learn quickly how important my eyes are (and how strange it is to see two roads ahead of you while driving...hint: close one eye.)

As a person who serves other people, I am determined to imagine that the person I am serving is a younger version of themselves. In reality, it is beneficial for me to imagine them being the most excellent kid in the school when they were young. Or maybe imagine them in their Spiderman or Dorothy from Wizard of Oz Halloween costume at the door saying, "Trick or treat!"

I can travel back through the history of a person by closely watching their eyes while we talk and imagining them younger again. Once I have done this, the watching of eyes, I have transformed my mind into a more empathetic person, no matter the age or demeanor they are. It makes me smile instantly and love them more. This is when I start to get very curious about a person. While I'm listening to them talk, I keep imagining them in the various scenarios they explain. Once curiosity takes over in the process of serving someone, everything gets easier. Learn about them. Dig deeper. "How long have you had this '51 Ford here?" See the movie in your mind. "What kind of car did your mom or dad drive when you were young?" Or, "What animals did you have growing up?" Then, be quiet and let them explain their memories. Then, ask more questions about what you see in your mind and hear from them as they talk. This could easily just be paraphrased as "getting into *the character*" (notice the other person!), which is one word different than you "getting into character" (thinking only of yourself.)

Really get into not only the positive person you want to project but also the other person in your play. This is a human with a library of memories standing in front of you. It is fascinating to me to imagine the life they have led leading up to the moment of this discussion. Play off of them (this is improv), and they will play off of you. This human connection dance doesn't happen very often, but when it does, people feel good. And when people feel good, you have either knowingly or unknowingly just served (&sold) them.

Remember, you love your product, but you really love your customers the most. And, they needed what you sold them because *you love what you are serving* (& selling) to the client and know it is suitable for their life. Or else you wouldn't be doing this work. Serve, and the net will appear (is that another tennis quote? Or maybe just a reference to a circus?) BTW, I love a circus, probably more than I love a parade. Try reading Ray Bradbury's *Something Wicked This Way Comes* to get in the same headspace on what I mean here... (for another time, put it on your list.)

When we take time to expand our minds, the connections we make with other people are more accessible.

How many interests do you have in your life? Try this quick **exercise** *to expand* the positive synapses (*and* **exorcise** *the negatives*) and get yourself in a more satisfying mindset. Then try to (a) do this same mindset exercise for each of the years of your life by writing down words that come to mind, one at a time or in a few word phrases, to relive your mindset from the year at hand. And then, (b) pick a word that you love, like Grandma, for instance, and write down the first things that come to your mind one word at a time. If you need to shut your eyes and meditate on these things, then do so. Take a 15-30 minute period to get in the *"Magnet Zone!"* (Another book again...) Let the words flow. You will exorcise the negatives later.

All of your most satisfying and frustrating memories will flood this zone. Your mind is the magnet; the memories are there, but now you are systematically organizing them. Keep a journal of all this. If it fills up, get another journal. I like to use the small black journals that are about the size of a book that can be bought at the drugstore. But they can be organized and look nice on a bookshelf in the future, so you have a consistent way to chronicle them. Get out your Magnet; it's time to work with and expand your mind!

By doing this exercise repeatedly, as time goes by, you will become a conversational magnet by keeping various fresh memories in your mind. Fresh memories are like fresh food; they taste better, and you want to savor them and serve them. The exercises will also increase the likelihood of being able to write your book someday. Wouldn't it be great to keep the library of your life experiences alive somewhere for posterity? When people die, it is as if a library was just burned down. Leave at least some of the library open for business and share your mindset with the world. This is how we can all grow more quickly through the generations.

Save all these notes and work with them to develop your mindset. If more negatives than positives come to mind when doing the exercises, then work to *exorcise* the negatives by going back to the Satisfaction vs. Frustration list. Revisit all your lists at least once every month or two to try to keep the habit alive.

Your ability to keep your mindset positive and robust is equivalent to understanding your foundation. Remodeling your life is a process. When we step into one room of our life at a time, we are able to think about what we love about the room and what we would love to change about the room. This is fun stuff. What's even more fun is enjoying your remodeled life, just like the new bathroom remodel. The newly remodeled mindset is always fun to share with others.

Are you able to become the author of your own life, write about it, make it feel more satisfying inside your mind, and then share your satisfaction with others? Most likely, you're already very good at sharing your frustrations. However, this process seems to introduce more anxiety and negativity into the world. Share the frustrations with yourself first, and work on exorcising negativity, not exercising negativity. At the same time, I want to capture the positive experiences, relish them, and share them.

The Memories List Exercise Example – (This was 18-20 minutes to grab my thoughts.... I may have drunk coffee in the process.)

Grandma House (*I do rhyming because it slows me down and makes me think more deeply about what I am really trying to convey to myself. Don't feel like you need to do this; just my jam...*) *write words, and you will see how fun it is...–*

Garden, sweet onion, asparagus, sink, smile, cool drink, listen, and think, cattle, the slew, starlings, and river, service, and smiling, duck hunting, cold shiver, motorbike, squirrels, alfalfa, train, midnight, the bed, sloped floor, window pane, curtain, and sprinklers, breeze blowing, the crickets, dresser drawers, closet, a doily, old trinkets, talking adults, the whispers, long-earing, prison nearby, the inmates, and fearing, washrag, the lava, junipers, oak, dust, covered porch, wheat farming, egg yolk, cold butter, toast, bacon, coffee, bait, mud suckers, fishing hook, chaffey, natives, the pies, massacre, gun, slew, frog, badger, rise sun, blue, harvest, moon, water, uncle, barnyard, hired hand daughter, wrangler, rodeo, roping, pony, gate, the chutes, sliver barn, old crony, grandma, perfume, wet dirt, play, pear tree, swingset, swimming, hay.

To me, this exercise can be much more fun than a video game and will provide me with more recent memories and concrete stories to share in the course of my service to others. What is more important to you than you? Spend time on you. Which means actually getting to know you. The more we know ourselves, the better we can serve others. The service (& sales) tend to increase with our conversational confidence and personal prowess. Dig into the positives from your past, and help yourself and others.

Helping others is sometimes the most challenging part. It does seem that sometimes others are unwilling to admit they need help. Have you heard the phrase, "Sometimes we are our own worst enemy?" Exorcise the past, exercise your ability to mine the positives in your life. I can tell you this – yes, people seem to be an obstacle to their growth. Both financially and personally, it is very tough for people to expand their horizons.

While those we serve have often become their own worst enemies when it comes to their same old habits, we are here to serve (& sell) them a better life for themselves. More on this later. All we can do is try to serve them, and formulate our thoughts, and be authentic. *Just say hello* and get to the serving (& sales) part.

OK, now it is time for the first major poem of the book. I love to rhyme. (Why do I love Eminem so much yet?) So, read this repeatedly and memorize words. We have an advantage: neither bees nor the birds can organize thoughts with their buzzing and songs; we're humans now people, and each person belongs.

Be near the game, and be on a championship team, and be a champion ready to be put in the game at all moments. You may not be the center of attention (Hint: Don't try to be either... remember, be a Chameleon, and blend in. But be the best, and know you are... that is enough to be a champion.)

Humble and Grateful

('Til Coach Calls My Name!") – *Joseph Devine*

——-//——-

Here on the sidelines

A champion's heart

My team in the game

But today, I won't start.

Where in the world

Could my life be less good?

Just about everywhere

Which is why I should

Be a bit humble

And be a strong heart.
The team may soon need me.
I do play a part
I'm grateful and tenacious, with my head in the game.
The mindset my friends
Neither fortune nor fame
Able to serve from the moment the coach calls
I've learned all the plays.
And I've busted down walls.
Brimming with gratitude
Boiling with "can."
I'm here with an attitude.
Of a blessed man
The "little me" 'chills.'
And the "poor me" stays home,
With the grace of Mandela
Repeating my poem...
"I will be the one
With the will to serve
I will be the one
When the ball starts to curve
I will be the one who exceeds my dreams.
I will be the one
With belief in my teams
I will be the one when the others fail.
I will be a hurricane, not just a gale.
I will undergo
Needed changes to grow
I will be the one, and that day, you will know.
All of my efforts
My will to move on,
Will never be wavering
All fear is now gone.

My fighting to push
Past adversity soon
Will cause me to jump
When they play that great tune
Jump, they may say, and "How high," I respond.
I will run right past the line; I will run way beyond.
The song, once again, that great tune in my mind
A chameleon I change, the global vision I find.
"We are the champions ..."
Wails Queen on the field
We are the ones
To charge forward, not yield
It's us there at sunset.
We will be there at dawn.
And when 'coach' calls my name
Watch my legend move on!"

Chapter 11

Be Authentic

Food, Art, Jewelry... The Real Thing

Why do you suppose we feel like we need jewelry? How did all that get started? I used to stand in front of my mom's jewelry box and marvel. And I like to see her wearing turquoise rocks and beads; she looks fabulous in that stuff. Being part of Indigenous people, I'm guessing she liked the feel of the weight of the stones, their shine, or the fact that these items were part of nature. I read somewhere that the first jewelry was shells that people strung together and traded. Then, as the thousands of years progressed, more precious metals melted down and became shiny and heavy items of worth. Soon, people began to value the metals and the minerals making up the jewelry just as much or more than the jewelry. What about the Egyptian pyramids? They did have a bit of a fetish for stuff, even when not living any longer.

Think about a diamond. How come people love to wear them and display their wealth and status with them? It's all a bit mysterious to me, but who am I to question this stuff? People have somehow collectively started to value things, minerals, and beautiful jewelry, sometimes just as much as they value themself or other people.

My daughters and wife do love clothing, too. When I worked in retail, I got it. I was infected by the desire to have the next best piece of clothing. It made me feel better always to be dressed in something different than the last time my friends saw me. But mostly, it was for me, for some reason... more therapy may be needed to get to the bottom of this one.

Anyway, it's strange how some people will even steal from and kill one another to get their hands on valuables. Others believe that a hard day's work should be spent buying these things for family, and maybe their posterity. Leaving behind material belongings is often a right of passage. "I earned it, and dammit, I can buy it," is a common refrain. It's all admirable, but sometimes it seems that this *pursuit of things* lacks a bit of authenticity. That's the point to dwell on.

Can I take all these things I've amassed to my grave (or an afterlife)? How badly do I need this beautiful home that makes me feel like I am living a "magazine life?" The stuff in the magazines is exciting because they put beautiful people in the scene, which makes us believe we will be beautiful if we get these things. <u>News flash:</u> *We are beautiful already.* It's all beautiful in a different way. Again, beauty seems to be a bit like pornography; we know it when we see it. But it is different than this as well. One person may think someone is beautiful, and another may not. The same is true with material things. Some care, some don't. And it all somehow makes sense that there are so many choices for us to make when buying something. Tastes are different in everything.

I love oysters, raw. Who else does? A ton of people. But who would never eat this uncooked, slimy and salty filter feeder? What's in the filter when it's complete? Maybe I should say I really like oysters because I may have made myself think about them for a few seconds too long. Anyway, I want to keep loving them.

And strangely, I'm one to like the beauty of a slug, or a blowfish, or bull thistle, or an orange. Many might agree with me on the orange. And, no matter what we look like, all of these things in the world that make up this fantastic planet are things of beauty. What is more beautiful, a French bulldog or a golden retriever? They probably cost about the same in some areas, and one is more popular than the other among specific populations. But doesn't it take all kinds of people to drive the economies of worth for all things? Honestly, it is up to the perceptions of the person admiring the intricacy of either of these to place a value judgment on either breed.

It's an issue, people. The problem is part of why we have such a tough time keeping our eye on the ball. The top one percent of the US Economy accounts for thirty-three percent of the nation's wealth. That means that 99% of us (damn near everyone) are all together worth half of what 1% of us is worth. Or some math close to that. What it really means is that things are too uneven with wealth; upon this, we can agree.

That stuff boggles my brain, and I'm not sure how it became like this, but my gut tells me to distribute more wealth to people who are in the lower and middle classes. Just sayin'.

So, in order to do this, more of us need to decide to buy less stuff that we don't need and focus on becoming more authentic. We could buy things that we need and instead invest the money that we spent on things we didn't need to increase our wealth. You ask, wait, does that actually work? Why yes, it does. If we could all learn this little trick, it would change the whole dynamic.

We have bought into buying. We buy things, and trinkets, and clothing, and trips...we buy collagen lips and pull fat from our hips... we eat more than we need then feel terrible soon...which brings on depression and sickness to ruin... marriages, lives, fall apart and then we... talk about negative things, so you see...it's time that we focus on positive stuff...and eat more authentic, maybe eat just enough. It's time that we work on our bodies and minds... to be the best 'us,' we must work our behinds... just a bit harder, do all the best things... and let our poor bodies be temples, not kings... for all of this stuff we are buying, consume... will soon lead to frustration when we're led to our tomb... Now, I'm just a guy with a regular brain, but why do we subject ourselves to such pain? I know if I turn to the mind that I knew when things were much more accessible, I was a kid, but I grew... I'd start to remember what matters, these people... the ones that have loved me, maybe prayed at the steeple... the lessons were there, the foundations for most... would give us a base and would help us not boast...by proving our worth from the things that we buy... why not be authentic? Be a regular guy (or girl, or them, & such...?)

There are always a ton of things we can buy out there to help free up our money for more innovative things. OK, back to the power bill (I'm slowly showing reality to you.)

Why are people insisting on paying rent for the power and letting it go up with inflation each year? Because that is the way it has always been. It is what our parents did because there was no other choice.

People! There is now another choice, and it has been for a few decades. You can actually pay off your power bill. You can own it, not rent it. You can invest the money you save...

Break it down now...

If you were to **(a)** take your permanently increasing power bill (let's say 5% increase yearly) and not hand it to a power company but instead make it part of your real estate (owning your Solar Panels to make power is an appurtenance on your real estate, and is now an asset instead of a liability) that increases by on average double every 10-12 years, then you could be converting your power bill (liability) to an asset that doubles every 10-12 years.

Another way is that if you give a $ 200-a-month power company money every year and increase it by 5% every year, they are taking money from you that you could have invested in your estate. If you were to **(b)** invest the $200 and the 5% compounded every year in an investment yielding a 5% return on average for the next 25 years, you would have $208,000 in your account. But, you needed power. So, to solve that part of the equation, you decide to get a $250 per month Solar Panel loan (including interest) to replace the power bill. In the same 25 years, that loan would have cost you $250 per month for 300 months (25 years), or $75,000.

So, to sum up this part, you **(c)** spent $75,000 to save $208,000, thus saving $133,000. Pretty good, huh? *But that's not all!* We will also throw in two doublings of the original purchase price ($50k) onto your roof, and it will double twice (because it is real estate that makes your power bill for you) over the next 25 years. Hint: Imagine you bought a car that makes its gas, but you have to pay off the vehicle first...this is how Solar works. Free power from the sun, but you need to pay off the panels before it is really free. So, this equity increase **(d)** adds $200,000 more dollars to your real estate value over the next 25 years. Which in the end means (wrapping this up here, so almost there...) you earned $200K in real estate value because you have a home with no power bill (it's like an addiction that kept going up in value, again because it is real estate...) and you earned $133,000 on your investments that you could make because you didn't have to pay an increasing power bill. Add those two together, and I just made you **$333,000** over the next 25 years on your current $200 power bill (and the power bill is now gone, too.)

Make sense? If not, read it slowly again. Please read it a third time. If you are still hesitant to invest in yourself, let your children read this (8-10-year-olds are the average age of kids who get the fact that $333k is way more than having zero of the $333k.) So, on behalf of the family, think long and hard about every financial decision together. It's a legacy decision. The kids will agree. If you don't believe me, ask them. Show them the math, and ask which is a better decision. You will see what I mean.

Most commonly, we hear people tell us, "We've done the math, and it doesn't make sense for us."

Question: Who in the tarnation is teaching financial math these days, and how come people say, "We did the math," and then decide not to save $333k over the next 25 years?

Again, I'm just sayin'. We have a long way to go for people to become the top 1% and to make decisions like the top 1% make. We need to do the actual math if we are ever going to make our money more important than our pride or our habits. We need to be authentic when we say, "I already did the math." Don't fall for your half-truths. Are they even half-truths? Why did you say you already did the math? Sometimes I just don't get it... A more positive way to say this last sentence (as all the workout gurus advise us to do...): Let's get it.

And wives, please ask your husbands as significant others to double-check your math. And vice versa... It is probably both of your money. Part of the role education plays in one's life is helping us to make better decisions. Be contemplative, and invite a learning mindset into your daily choices. "Not interested" is an admission that one isn't curious to learn. "I already did the math" is an admission that you'd somewhat exaggerate just to make a point than get educated. Break these habits, please, because if you do so, you will look more trustworthy and open to learning. Why would one not consider saying, "Show me the math; I'd love to see how you calculate the savings?" Use phrases that encourage learning in your daily lives.

Let's truly get it. (And if you're still saying, I don't get it, then read the math problem above ten more times in a row.) This is what I had to do to become the valedictorian of my high school. I was not more intelligent than other people. I did get a four-year scholarship but did not get a degree. I chose to live a different path. I wasn't afraid of hard work. I knew I could succeed with hard work. The fact is, I had to work ten times harder (or at least several times harder) to read and re-read and re-read and re-read and re-read and re-read the concepts I was studying in order to make sure they stuck in my noggin. Try it. Dig in harder. You can do it. Let's get it.

And one last significant point here. A friend of mine at my daughter's swim meet recently told me his thoughts on what has gone awry in America. It all made perfect sense to me. In essence, he was recapping what we have mostly all endured.

- We were told we needed to go to school to succeed.
- We were told to raise our hand at school.
- We were told to make sure to do our homework, even when we didn't like the subject.
- We were told we needed to get a college degree if we were ever to amount to anything.
- We bought into a system where we rack up hundreds of thousands of debt to get the degree.
- We make sure to get a job that pays more than the average with our degree.
- Our bosses want us to stay in line and follow the system (raise your hand...)
- We endure an economy where prices are rising for us all faster than our incomes.

- The company does better than we do.
- Incomes for the upper class increased, while those of the lower and middle classes stagnated and dropped.
- We decided two incomes are needed to keep up with the inflation and weakening dollar.
- So both work (or single mothers and fathers are in an even more impossible boat) to be able to make ends meet.
- We move further away from where we work to afford life where we live.
- We consume more fossil fuels (battery cars are on the rise, but Lithium is not great for the world either) and increase CO_2 in the atmosphere by driving further.
- We threaten the environment with our CO_2 footprint, our mining, our consumption, etc.
- We pay more to clean up the environment.
- We tend toward organic food and beverages to reduce environmental damage and increase our chances of better health, but we pay more for doing so.
- We have to choose between our children's health and the environment every day.
- We imperil our health by buying what we are forced to eat when we lack the money to buy the more expensive organic food.
- We have to pay more for health insurance and drugs due to the sicknesses caused by the environment, living conditions, and diet.
- We vote and vote again for people who are unwilling to work with one another.
- We fear the other voting party, so we don't dialogue as much, or mostly anywhere it seems…
- We criticize, judge, and divide one another rather than work to unite our efforts and resources toward a common goal.

- We allow the negatives to outweigh the positives.
- We become negative.
- We get therapy for hopelessness.
- We seek comfort in sex and drugs.
- We increase the amount of unwanted pregnancies.
- We create more illegal activity to offset the impossible situation.
- We break families apart to offset the impossible situation.
- We kill more children and inmates to offset our poor decision-making.
- We pass regressive laws to allow ourselves to have more to fight about rather than less.
- We point the finger at people of different races, colors, and sexual persuasions and make them believe they are the reasons for all the problems.
- We reduce our circle of trust in others.
- We forget that when we point the finger at someone else, three fingers are pointing back at ourselves... and it leaves us with an unattended thumb, which can be a considerable problem (just a side note, but worth pondering...)

I could keep writing this circadian rhythmic list for days or months on end if I tried. It seems that people have gotten on each other's last nerve. And this brings us back to why people will say they "did the math already, and it doesn't work for our budget and family..."

Thank you to my friend Jason for zeroing me in on the problem. Half the time, I get so focused on the solution for the issues that I don't sit and survey the full depth and breadth of the problems we face.

I know many of you reading this book could add hundreds of topic points where we could do better. I would love to hear up to 500 words on my Substack (josephdevine.stubstack.com) about your hopes for America and the World. If they are productive comments, I will respond. If they are mean or negative, I will block you from contributing in the future. There are enough negatives in the world without my process adding any more. Positives and solutions are good contributions to our human condition. Together, we can do better. Be authentic. Be a good meal. Don't draw too much attention to yourself, but instead, focus on how you can be more humble, grateful, and contributory to the world you were born into. Please! And, Thank you.

Holy crap. We need to get more positive, start working together, and get our acts together. We are way more talented than we have allowed ourselves to believe. Our creativity as humans in the 21st century is off the charts. By looking at the world we live in, our politics and our tendency toward divisive behavior, one wouldn't know it (until one dug a bit deeper…). Let's dig deep and understand each other better to better serve (& sell) the best of one another to each other.

Make long-term decisions (and really do the math when you say you've done the math…)

Thanks again for joining me in this chapter of our journey. I couldn't do it without you all.

What do we mean when we say we want to make the world a better place, but then we continue to display our same old habits that are potentially part of the problem?

This book is about growth. It is for you. I hope that you will take to heart the topics I'm introducing in this book about service (& sales) and make good on a commitment to do your part. Let's get down on it (get your back up off the wall, dance, come on!) Speaking of dance, I also really, really love Frankie Goes to Hollywood! This was a pivotal album for me in the middle nineteen eighties. What music makes you feel good and makes you want to share yourself with others? Write a song, a poem, or a musical or play. Sell yourself to the world. Please share your ideas with us all. We want to hear them and embrace them, and we want them to flow freely.

Again... Music folks.

Chapter 12

Conception

All Sales is Sexy... Kind of

That infant we met in the first chapter had a few good trimesters to chill before "hitting the ground." My Dad, being the horse veterinarian, used to call it that when the foal was born. There's always a different way to look at things. Isn't it amazing that twenty-three chromosomes have a date with another twenty-three, and then there is this odd little forty-six being living its secret life inside another person for an entire school year?

From the moments before the quarterback calls an audible and takes the hike, there was a full-service sales job in motion to go for the touchdown. And there is always a different mood before conception. But there is always a sales job. Who loves Joe Cocker? *You Are So Beautiful*, the 1974 version, may be one person's style, or perhaps *You Can Leave Your Hat On* from 9 ½ Weeks, Kim Bassinger and Mickey Roarke is another's modus operandum. "I think I've been hypnotized...How did you know I'd respond to you the way I have?" Kim Basinger's character asks. And Mickey Roarkes replies, " I saw myself in you."

Darn, it's a good movie. That is a helluva line there, too. It hit me right at the perfect time. When I was twenty, I was very attracted to the opposite sex, and this movie pulled me straight toward wanting to buy a CD player, among other things. Moreso, I learned to love Joe Cocker from this movie. How did this movie get me so fired up? It was selling sex, and I was buying. Watch the trailer again sometime, the one with his song. I got deeper into wanting to be part of the music scene from the moment I saw this movie. I thought it would be my ticket to more experiences like the movie showed. Sex sells. And music works really well when it comes to planning a good conception.

Well, it doesn't really work exactly like this, but when one lets go and becomes a person in the moment, a connection starts to happen.

Now, this doesn't mean we need to pursue relationships from a sexual perspective. In fact, it doesn't mean we need to want to have something or someone. What it means is that we want to be signifi-cant in our relations with other people. If someone sees you are seeking to create a relationship just to get something yourself, they can often see it a mile away and quickly.

So, if you are trying to sell someone, they will smell it. Then, they will resist and work to find ways to get away from you. But suppose you instead seek to understand more about the person (thank you, Steven Covey!) and take it a step further, meaning, really seek to know about the person's surroundings, their family, their pain points, their budget issues, or you name it. In that case, you are on the road to being able to get them to drop their guard and see you as someone they can trust.

Remember, don't try to get them to trust you if, in fact, you are not trustworthy. This is a mistake. This is like the one-night stand, and it often doesn't feel so good the next day. Lord knows we don't need the sale to be canceled within three days of the right of decision. There's nothing more demoralizing than this one... Enter stage left, buyer's remorse. Who wants the one-night stand sale? Once you've had a few of them or too many of them, you start to feel poorly about yourself. You feel as though you are quickly sold and regretful that you didn't see it coming. Sadly, you start to lose your self-confidence, which then works against your ability to make the next sale happen. The worst thing is for the hunted one to feel as though they aren't being seen as a person to be cared about. If the salesman is hunting, the chances are good that the customer doesn't want to be the prey. They run away, or they fight you. When we do a quick sale, with seduction as our tool, it will come back to bite us. Ask Little Red Riding Hood about this.

However, if we look at the person as though we genuinely care about them, then everything starts to go our way smoothly. If we try to understand the person and realize that this thing we are trying to show them wouldn't be good for their situation, then we must let them know that it wouldn't be the right thing for their situation.

Sometimes, the one-night stand or the wham-bam sale is consensual. And in sales, this is called "the laydown." For instance: *"My friend Ken said you would be the perfect person to service me. I totally trust that he knows what I want, so where do I sign to get this thing moving forward?"* That seemed pretty simple, huh? What if sales were really like this? After a while, it wouldn't be fun. I can tell you this from experience.

Instead, we desire a deeper relationship. One with a foundation from a position of understanding one another. Will this relationship or service you are trying to suggest to me be good for me? What about you and your product will make my life better? I don't want to end up married to the wrong product. Nobody really does.

When it comes to a big-ticket item (the more significant the item, the more complex the sale), like a car, a home, or solar panels, we want to have a deeper understanding of what we are getting into. Foreplay. Plenty of it. And not for seduction's sake, but for caring and kindness' sake. This is because we want to know who we are getting into bed with; we want to trust this person entirely. We want to know if this person and this company and this product they represent will be able to give us the service we need; that will solve my problem.

If you are in business for a laydown buyer, then look for a sales training model that is different from what I am suggesting.

There is another mindset that some sales teams employ. That is the hand-off strategy. This type of salesperson will provide information and hand off the decision to the buyer. This is a passive approach, which works only slightly better than waiting for the laydown.

Then there are the prayer-based people in a sales mindset. They want to sell stuff, but they don't really want to do the work to get things done. It actually takes loads of work to get stuff done, and you have to want to get things done. If you would instead get into sales and then pray that it works for you because you are in the business, then once again, you're likely praying up the wrong tree.

People who get into sales for money would be well advised to remember that it takes diligent and honest work to make money happen. And it can quickly end if one starts to take shortcuts. This I do well know.

Although some people in sales do have a sixth sense and seem to understand where to be in order for sales to fall into their laps, again, this is passive. When I was younger, I could hang out in the best bar in town (I had done so when I was young) and wait for an attractive woman to walk in, then conjure up a way to appeal to their inner chameleon with my inner chameleon. I think you can feel the same mood welling up inside yourself if you remember back to those days. But after a while, most of us agree that we have grown tired of trying to attract sales this way. When the head hits the pillow, primarie is primarily looking for someone to spend some more time with and enjoy the time we are spending with them.

I was at the parents of my daughter's home the other night to pick up my daughter after they played on the dock in the neighborhood for a hot summer afternoon. By evening, the couple was out watching the remnants of the sunset and invited me to sit down on the deck and look at the lake. It was a perfectly still evening, and the kids were finishing up playing but not quite ready to leave. They offered me a glass of whiskey. And it is at times like these that I would sometimes wish I hadn't stopped drinking thirty years earlier, but that flash of thought passed in a few seconds, the same as it had hundreds of times for that same thirty years. A clear mind is always best, for sure.

As we began to talk, we started to learn more about each other. We had known each other through the school and kids for years already but had never really talked about much different than the children. Even a year earlier, I had told them how great the school my older daughters attended was, and they were happy to learn about it and hadn't heard of it before. Coincidentally, his daughter will be going to the same school (selling even when not trying to sell...we love to share good things!)

We got on the subject of homes and then the father's work. I was fascinated by his work in the field of AI and ChatGPT. He told me how it had been happening for many years before any of us heard of it. The development stage was highly controversial and unlocked a whole new generation of young people who were hard at work to make this industry come to life. There is always some new disruptive technology right around the corner. And when it is born or comes to pass, there is often a whole new wave of fear and anxiety from those whose jobs it may adversely affect. And a whole new wave of sales is needed to service the industry itself.

This is undoubtedly the case in his field. He spoke for at least fifteen minutes before he dawned on me that he wasn't really sure what I did for a living. He then pivoted from himself to me. I said one sentence about my work in Solar, and that was going to be it. I have an uncomfortable feeling trying to do business with family or friends. It can often end in "hurt feelings & mayhem," as my brother likes to say. Be wary of friends and family selling, for sure (another book, again.)

But his curiosity was piqued, and he kept asking more about it. Soon, it came out that he had been considering Solar for his home, and I wanted to know if I thought it would work for him. We walked around the house, looking at various challenges with the shape and orientation, and the position of several trees, and decided that it would be feasible to make it happen for him; and, being a builder in the past, I did have to let him know about some of the ways we could overcome another problem he had been having with his insulation. Poor insulation was at the root of his elevated electric bill. All things are tied together and relate to one another when it comes to deciding to change parts of a home—electrical leads to discussions of gas and global warming. Hot Planet leads to a debate on children and their grandkids. Depressing talk leads back to reality. Reality will soon lead to the inability to burn gas in the coming decades. Gas leads to HVAC questions, which then leads to summer and winter norms for the home, which then leads to insulation, which then leads to windows, and ultimately, back to the budget: round and round. Then, we focus on the discussion. He wants to get a quote for his home, and soon, I am going against my own guarded rule of working with a friend or someone reasonably close. But they do need the help. Just remember, this is about service and helping them not to get taken advantage of by someone else. We want the best for all these people, as well as our friends and family.

Building and sales belong together, but not too close together. If a person is addicted to money, it can be easy to make ideas that make people want to spend their money. The problem is this addicted person isn't thinking about the best interests of the home or the homeowner. Instead, too often, they try to solve their money problems and desire to make another sale. Red Flag here...

If we only want to serve the person and do what is best for them, then we don't have to let ourselves get in the way of our service. Unless we are going for the seduction and the wham-bam moment (which we should have gotten out of our system after our first couple of one-night stands), then it would be best to revert to our tennis game. Just volley the ball back and forth until we finish one game or set. And after several "love-love" moments, a few ad-ins and a few ad-outs, we are ready for the match to end. If we play fair the whole time, then we want to play again. That is a summary of both service (&sales) and tennis. Keep volleying, and have fun. It is a game for a lifetime, just like a marriage and a relationship.

Who wants to play tennis with someone who is poor at sport or who is stretching the rules? Better yet, who wants to have a life with someone that doesn't love them? Who among us wishes they had not bought the product they did? When this happens, there are always bad reviews. Negativity starts to well up in and around this person, and ultimately, their dissatisfaction with their choice becomes a wedge that makes others not want to be around them. Sometimes, they don't want to be around themselves, which is very sad. Who wants to be part of all this kind of malarky? What if we were to treat everyone nicely and want the best for them? I sense that the health and wealth of the person who follows the "treat them nicely" mantra will not only be treated nicely themselves but also enjoy better health and wealth. Those who serve us treat us nicely. Don't use people as your *sales toy*.

Seriously, try this: just be positive, and even pretend to be positive when you think you can't allow yourself to act positively. Be nice, and enjoy the other person. For negative-minded people, the last sentence can be the toughest one to embrace. "Being nice won't fix these problems," the negative-minded person may say. Are they then trying to tell the inverse of their statement, which is essentially, "Being mean will fix these problems!" I'm not sure, but the reason I am not sure is that I can't usually identify with a person with a negative mindset.

Enough about that. Just be nice.

OK, let's say we look at conception again. We sometimes want to go into business with the conception of a new alliance as the end goal. And when it works, this beautiful new product or relationship we have spawned is a game changer. Why did we want this baby? Why did we want something different that wasn't yet in our life to be in our life? This is the over-arching question about why people buy things. Usually, people feel emotionally empty, or sometimes they feel out of control. And sometimes, people want to fulfill their inner animal drive. With purchases that affect the larger budget of one's life, it tends to be the out-of-control feeling that is at stake. A home, a car, a significant investment, a baby, Solar panels, or a new roof hits people at the core. On the one hand, they know they need to change their current situation, yet on the other hand, they aren't sure how to go about it or what would be best for them in the long run.

Let Them Be – This is where serving up knowledge and guidance come into the picture. As salespeople, we aren't going to fix someone's life, and we aren't going to decide for them. It has to be organically mined from the depths of the person's situation. The buyer knows best. I'm afraid I have to disagree with the adage, "The customer is always right." A more accurate statement may be, "Always treat the customer right." They may be incorrect when they are making their points or objections, but if we treat them correctly for a little bit while they voice their case, our inherent inner chameleon will allow the "customer just to be..." And this is the end goal. Let them be them. Help them be them. Watch them be them. Hear them, be them. Smile at them. Talk with them. Understand them. Thank them. *"Them's our customers!"*

Back to sex. Now, maybe after the big moments, the service (& sale), there actually is conception, and maybe not. But in history, the whole reason attraction is occurring in its natural habitat (which is all day, all over the world) is so that human beings will procreate. Advertising one's wares to others is at the root of sales. Helping them know why they need our wares is how conception is more likely. But when one person meets another, if there is a feeling that makes both people feel not quite right, realize that every peacock doesn't find every hen attractive. Yet, the peacock needs several mates to be satisfied. Not all animals are the same, but peacocks like getting it on and naturally do it with many partners. So, in a way, the peacock is a good metaphor for the salesperson.

Why do we need sex? It may be closely related to why we need to serve. Serving others makes us feel good. Sex makes us feel good (although, of course, there are exceptions for both.)

All these words keep floating around in my mind, so that I will write them.

Love, love, service. Sex is service; service is sex. Love is sex; love is service. Tennis is love. Sales is tennis. We volley, and strangely, love uses mainly the same letters as a volley. Back and forth. Up and down. In and out. Here and there. This and that. Ying and Yang. Self service. Self-love. Service above self. Love it. OK, enough. This is how my mind gets sometimes. I know it is tough to figure out what we are supposed to do with our lives, but I am pretty sure it involves everything in the last paragraph, except maybe tennis. And even then, we could play a quick game of couples to show our love for the game. Ah, heck, I think I may need to start a new chapter to get out of this loop. Love what you sell, love yourself, love your customer, and conceive the sale. Stay in the relationship, and have as many partners as you need to pay for the ties... Get it? It's tough being a peacock, but I guess that's sales. There.

Chapter 13

Create Curiosity First

Why is this sexy?

One of my favorite music videos is by Yves LaRoc. *Rise*. If you're anything like me, you will want to watch this or watch a minute of it before you move on to the next task. Or even better yet, the whole thing.

If you actually did take a look at it, then maybe you're a curious person. If you watched it all the way to the end, you may be more like me than you think. I not only love the video but also love its message.

This girl in the video is curious about others she sees doing some extreme jump rope to the beat of the song. The beat of a song is a whole other subject (another book I'm writing, but staying focused here...). In the womb, before the baby in chapter one was experiencing the rhythm of life on the outside, there was a heartbeat soothing them (probably not yet) on the inside. Take a minute of quiet and think of the heartbeat. Touch your heartbeat. If everything is quiet and you are in tune with your heart, you are experiencing glimpses of that memory that was created for you by two things...(a) A Creator (or something you believe in...) and (b) sex.

So we progress. Everything is about progression. If we experience the world in a lineal manner, we are living the life we were meant to live. We learn things one step at a time. We hear thousands of beats and fantastic music as we grow, and it touches our hearts. Why? That is the question for you to answer. And many people are curious enough about themselves to try to dig deeper into the bearing ground to find it. We talked about the foundation before, but the bearing ground is the womb that housed and nourished us from the very beginning. That's where the magic happens.

I once had a stone guy (that's what we call the hard surfaces, granite, soapstone, etc.) tell me that construction is like the A, B, and C's. When a new person starts in the business, we need to teach them about A; then, when they learn plenty and progress forward on that subject, it's time to move to B. So, the service is a lot like this concept. If we can learn to be served and sustained by the bearing ground (mom) first, we can then progress to the next step. How many years does it take to learn how to be served? There should be at least a few, maybe more for some than others. Yet, at some point, we move on to the finer points of serving others.

At the age of 3 or 4 years old, my Dad had a list of chores for me to do. The way he approached things was to pay me for my time and my age per month. When I turned five years old, my monthly allowance grew from $4 to $5. My first raise was a 25% increase... Nice.

Dad wanted us to learn to work and would have us do work every day after school for his veterinary business and even for his friends. This was a progression from working only for the family to working for others. This is when service starts. When we were working for Dad, we were serving his business clients. By this point, we are likely up to the letter E in the alphabet. Our brains are 90% formed by now for the basics of how to communicate with others, but there is an untapped reservoir of learning yet to be achieved. Everyone has a different learning and growing pace. I suspect that the earlier one starts serving, the more curious one becomes. Someday, a researcher will dig further into this concept, but I will let them do a proper study that we can all learn from (again, this stuff is all ancient but worth considering.)

My theories of my everyday observations are mostly just that. Most of us have a ton of everyday observations, and then some like to relate one observation to another as a way to remember better and gain a deeper understanding of the world around us. These people are curious (mostly all people, and less the rest, "Don't call me Leslie... Airplane.)

Then we go off to school. Now, there are many other boys and girls in the class, and we are in the process of rounding out our ability to communicate with others through collaboration. The teacher collaborates with us, piquing our curiosity, and the students throw out answers when the teacher asks. Volley a question and hit it back. Tennis again. Why did they settle on the word "service" in tennis anyway? I'm not sure, but it is a great way to see our curiosity in action. For some, the game is boring. Now it's time to ask yourself another question... Was that how school seemed to me? Some think certain subjects in school are boring. Others may love the same subject. The whole school system was put together to give us structure and a foundation upon which to work. It is the foundation for which we then let our curiosity go to work. Maybe if the institution of education would work earlier and more diligently to cater to our innate desire to serve one another, there could be outcomes that allow students to exercise their curiosity and their unique talents comprehensively and fluidly. This could be accomplished through integration with non-profit organizations or maybe internship programs for students to learn various trades earlier in their lives. Having children see work or *Service* through a process of allowing them to be closer to those adults conducting day-to-day work in the world would almost certainly increase the capacity for our children to learn better how to work themselves.

I love the schools because there is an environment of daily growth, or progression, inherent in the process of learning. Again, *progression and process.* These concepts are equivalent to learning how to serve. If we watch others serve from a young age, we are more likely to pick up on the innate desire to serve. The truth is, everything in this paragraph is critical to the groundwork for learning how to increase our service (& sales.)

A blend of work and becoming educated daily is how service will expand in our businesses and lives. So why is this so important? I'm not totally sure. However, it seems like a solid concept to embrace. Anything I've ever become better at involved putting in the reps. When I have worked at something, my desire to become better at it has increased. The desire to understand stems from the desire to work, and vice versa. Work and learn. Learn and work. This means we need to seek out growth actively, and when we do, our curiosity grows.

What is wrong with me? If I look back on my life, I realize that for much of my early life, I wanted to become a veterinarian like my father. Sometimes, I also thought it would be fun to be a teacher because I love to learn by myself. But, after going to college for one year on a full four-year academic scholarship, I had an allergy appointment with a doctor at the University of Washington School of Medicine.

It was a simple enough appointment because I had been a kid with allergies my whole life. My Dad was a horse doctor, so I also wanted to become one. At the appointment that day, my allergist asked me, "Why do you want to be sick for the rest of your life when you're going into a field of medicine? You know you're terribly allergic to horses; it just seems like you may want to think about doing something that isn't going to make you sick."

It was a reasonably logical question, as doctors seem to be known for asking. Why do all of the questions about "why" seem to get my thinking so much? What do I want to do if I don't become a horse vet? I hadn't ever thought of this because my life had been progressing in one direction, and to change the direction would be new and different. Making a pivot (as we call it in sales and basketball) requires practice and some introspection. The scientific method started to kick in at this point for me. If not this, then what? The questions began to race through my mind.

The scientific method would require me to create a new hypothesis about myself. Up to this point, I had observed (a) things I chose to do, I typically ended up being reasonably talented at, and (b) it was comforting to think back about the parts in my life that made me feel satisfied and sound, so maybe it was a good idea to try to do some of these things in adulthood.

Inventing one's self takes creativity. Just because nobody has taken your exact path before doesn't mean that you're unable to create your idea of how to live your life.

My curiosity started to make me curious and took over my drive to blaze a new trail. By leaving college, I would now be in a new world of daily survival. When the process of bypassing the typical college route culminates in starting a new direction, it can be daunting and complex.

Imagine you are trying to reinvent yourself after years of habit and dedication leading you through the typical institutional school system. For me, this fruit salad, of course, had given some variation to my life, but it hadn't actually prepared me for what would come next. At first, after college, I tried several different avenues to enable money to start flowing. I tried selling a product named Aqua Fresh. I tried selling term insurance. I tried taking time off from both work and school. And I tried to work more for my Dad. None of these ideas seemed fulfilling to me.

Then, one day, I applied to work at the local seafood restaurant, and this was the point at which I blossomed into the service engine that would switch me into high gear. I loved how it felt to clean up after people. I loved how it felt to exceed the expectations of the service when I was a busboy. I wanted to be faster and better conditioned than the others. What I yearned for and was receiving was a job that would give me purpose. In the service and hospitality industry, I found what I sought. I progressed near my twenty-first birthday to bartending. This was the job I felt most at home in. I was able to talk with the guests I served well into the night and felt myself becoming part of the support system of their lives. Giving ones' self to others is a privilege that is difficult to replicate. Service to these same people comes in all manners.

If curiosity hadn't been alive and well, I may not have learned that I wanted to be not only good but better than most who had ever done my position.

Still progressing, I felt as though I were maybe up to the letter H in my progression. Hospitality.

Giving excellent bedside manners to those we serve is what makes them feel good. Making them feel cared for, heard, and heralded as essential and loved is the simple way to take care of others. Have you ever been sold versus served?

The person who tries to "sell" another is the person who is thinking for himself. The person who tries to **"serve"** another is the person that others think of from then on. This is the person that others want to be around. This is the person who draws the inner chameleon out of others. This is the person who wants the best for others. This is the person who puts others in a good mood. This is the person who says hello to others each day. This is the person that smiles at others all day long. This is the person who begins an interaction with a smile and ends it ever more warmly than it started. This is the person that reminds us of a friend or loved one. This is the friend. *This is the loved one.*

Be curious about each other, and make the day better for someone else. There is no time like now. Remember this. There is no time like now.

Curiosity is sexy. Try to be more curious, and you will rise to levels you haven't before in all facets of your life. Ask questions of others. Ask about them and what they think. Ask about how you can help them solve their problem. It is magnetic. It is sexy.

Chapter 14

Foreplay

The Frog, The Stalker, the Dreamer and the Doer

We loved with a love that was more than love. - Edgar Allen Poe.

Be honest, brutally honest. That is what's going to maintain relationships (& sales...) - Lauryn Hill

I love these two quotes (I added sales to the second one, but think about it!)

When the person walks into the bar that is attractive to you, what does it do to your body and mind? For most people, memories of moments like these are seared into our minds. The romantic attraction for a stranger upon first seeing the stranger is pretty rare. This feeling isn't likely to happen more than a few times in one's life (debatable...), And even more rarely, it ends up having a possibility of becoming something deeper and more meaningful. Yet, people go to the bar and wait. The people who like to fish know this feeling. There's going to be a lunker out there. Patience is a virtue. The fishermen are sometimes like stalkers.

However, to be successful in sales, we can't just spend our lives in a bar or a sandbar, casting for possibilities. Success happens when we proceed with intent in life. Success occurs when we proceed. Proceed.

The Frog, The Stalker, the Dreamer and the Doer - (future kids book here.) Are you the type of person who would walk up to that person in the bar whom you just met and say something to them? I refer to this type of person as the frog. That is, when the fly comes near to the frog, it has to stick out its tongue. The critter is just wired that way. We are all wired in some way. At times, we are awkward, but what the heck? "I've got a little frog in me... Would you like a little?" (Kidding, that was a joke in the bars on St. Patrick's Day; substitute the world Irish for frog.) Or maybe you are the type of person who would watch them for a while and see how they behave with friends they came to the bar with, then perhaps start thinking about things you could say to impress the person. How could you possibly devise a strategy to be with this person for the rest of your life?

There have been thousands of stories written about this age-old dilemma. In sales, we call this person the stalker. (Enter Frank, this is your shoutout...) Or maybe you're more of a dreamer who wishes you could meet the person but doesn't have the impulse to convert the dream into an actual life exchange with the other person. This person wants to be brave but has certain blocks in the mind that prevent forward motion and action from happening at the moment.

Know who you are. Visualize how you will handle your daily interactions with people throughout the day, then proceed with intent.

Is it possible to be partly all three of these? Have you ever even thought about stalking someone? If you're in sales, you have. You have plotted, strategized, and tried to become a great chess player to ensure the sale becomes a reality.

As a stalker, what if you were to ask yourself, how can what I have to offer help make this person's life better? This thought process takes time to develop. The purpose of this book is to help us become more thoughtful and to act.

Why do we want to help others? Well, in the case of the person walking into the bar, the answer is usually first and foremost to help ourselves. Something inside the beautiful person we see is drawing us to them. Something is telling us that we need them. It's not a whole lot different than that feeling that arose in us when reading chapter one. It's a primal magnetic pull that is making our whole being desire something or someone else. So, does the sales stalker need something or someone? I would say yes. There is an internal drive for money or winning or even self-fulfillment that is driving the sale. But the best sales stalkers want to serve. Bam!

When service steps into the picture or onto the stage, all else falls together like lovers in an embrace. Rather than asking ourselves, "How can I get that person or thing that just came into my view," what if we were to ask ourselves, "How can I serve that person that just came into my view?" Bam! Again, maybe this is the whole mindset shift you were looking for in your life. Book over. No...

After spending years serving others, only one time in my life can I say that the person I met in the bar was more than just another person to serve. It is rare to meet the love of your life. But if that love could then translate into a love for other people as well, meaning you treated all others you meet with a regard that is similar to that for those in your life you most love, you would be on the path to enjoying the type of love, and the type of success described in the Poe quote above.

Side story. I have interviewed thousands of people in my life. I love interviewing people. I love 99% of Charlie Rose and have been a lifelong fan of his. (The other one percent will be in a different book about failure and adversity.) But bear with me here. His ability to draw deep conversations out of people is nearly unparalleled. He is a fantastic interrogator and able to help people dig into their pasts to find out how they became who they are. Watch some episodes if you haven't already. Ask yourself, "How could I become more like the part of the Rose we love?" Every rose has its thorns. Let's focus on the rose.

In early 1994, a rose walked into a bar I was managing. Her friend had invited her for an interview with me because I was looking for a bartender. When I arrived at the top of the stairs in the Waterfront restaurant in downtown Kirkland and saw her eyes, that feeling happened. This moment is seared into my mind. Peter Gabriel's song In Your Eyes flashed through my being...*I see the light and the heat. Oh, I want to be that complete. I want to touch the light, the heat I see in your eyes.*

When a body vibrates and feels yearning, it is that moment. In chapter one, the baby is at that moment. Indescribably connecting with another is that moment.

So how do we come closer to that moment when we see other people? I feel as though we are pack animals. If a wolf strays from the pack for days into another valley or wood, there is a celebration when it reunites with the pack. There is a joy that exudes from all the members of the pack. All of the wolves feel happier and more satisfied at home. When we are together, we are better. When we see each other as part of the pack, we are better. When we feel at home, we are better. When we see the eyes and the person inside the gaze of those eyes, we are better. Because of each other, we are better.

Service – Wait, that's not work. When we connect, we are not only better, but we are also living. Whether you are a frog, a stalker, or a dreamer, break down the perceived barriers inside your mind and reach out for another. But you must be a doer. We need a new word for work here; it's overused. How about *service?* Work to serve and worship one another and your higher power in order to achieve growth and survive.

The girl in the bar didn't actually know how to bartend, so in a sense (and in most bar owners' minds), she wasn't qualified. Me? I hired her. I told her, "I will teach you how to bartend, no worries." We have been married for 27 years and have three beautiful daughters. She could mix a mean cocktail, knows how to connect, and is the love of my life.

When does connection happen? When you make it happen. We don't know what we don't know. So, how do we then start to learn? We get curious. We connect. We listen to each other and solve each other's problems. We walk into the bar, and we find something that makes us better; then, we make our way back to the pack.

If we are in sales, then we get up each day, feed ourselves, stay organized, and pursue the world. We lower our defenses. We use our instincts (the frog) to use our will to overcome and to survive, and we make stuff happen. Work is only work if you have the mindset that you are working. If you are living, connecting, and loving, you are growing. This is your success. The money that you seek will fall into your lap. Maybe even the love you seek will fall into your lap (I had to say that one...), And when that happens, damn, it feels good. Sing it, Eminem, "Can I get a witness? (hell yeah!)

Why do we wait so long to change our mindset? When it came to the applicant for a bartender who had no experience, I was the frog, the stalker, and the dreamer. I knew I could work to do whatever needed to happen to achieve the dream. And now, I am living and loving my dreams every day.

What do you want in your life? If you want to be loved, then go live. If you want to be served, it takes a service mindset. Those with all the money seem to have an easier time purchasing their services. We, too, can do the same, but we first must serve ourselves and, above all, serve others. "Can I get a follow? Let's get these dinners out of the window!"

Be a rose, grab a rose, smell a rose, and do it. What a blast to be alive. Take time to smell each other.

Chapter 15

Looking Like a Rockstar

When you're dumb as a rock...

"Hey now, you're an all-star, get your game on, go play...Hey now, you're a Rock Star; get the show on and get paid!" Thank you, Smash Mouth.

It's a good song and inspirational for the kids, yet it's not totally consistent with getting paid. We pay ourselves through our habits and our investments in our future.

I have met so many young salespeople who want to look like a rockstar (successful, flush with money...) to make it seem like they are great salespersons. Then they flush the cash. When one tries to give the impression that one is wealthy when that isn't the case, one could be characterized as borderline dumb. Because money is scarce, it is critical to success to have the money one has saved because stuff happens. Be sensible when purchasing the things in your life that are wants instead of needs. You will need much more money than you realize in the future. And the future is unpredictable. As Dave Ramsey proclaims, if one has an emergency fund, they are less likely to have an emergency. Be the one to help others in an emergency. If you don't have an emergency fund, you will have more emergencies.

It took me quite a few years to come to this conclusion about saving and not wasting funds. If I had learned the lesson earlier, I would have been able to save and invest so much more money than I actually did. Sometimes, this thought nearly makes me want to roll over and play dead.

You will make money in sales. You may make a ton of money in sales. Sales is one of the top-earning professions in the world, and your desire to be part of this sector is a precursor to your ability to learn the power of serving others. Learn. Serve others. These actions bring success. Money isn't everything, but the lack of it is nothing. Spending it wisely is a great way to ensure you're able to get better and better jobs in the future. Others who see your success and your resulting calm and confident demeanor will want to emulate your habits. You will be the one who is able to help others in need, and conversely, you will need to help others who you meet upon your chosen path.

The Danger Zone - Overspending is not only dumb but dangerous to your future. Some of the top salespeople enjoy creating this aura of money around them so that other people will believe their success is giving them the freedom to purchase whatever they want. What are we doing here, people? Are the people who do business with us more likely to buy the snake oil or essential things we sell if we are pretending to be someone we aren't with our fashion choices? I have noticed that those selling snake oil will do creative tricks to distract the buyer from seeing the truth. The *things* may very well be tricks. A company tricks us into *needing* the flashy or trendy product, and then we fall for the trick and become complicit and lose the authenticity we once had.

Have you ever sat at a table with a piece of paper and added up the cost of the fashion splurges you have embarked upon? Macklemore and Ryan Lewis, bring it...Check out the *Thrift Shop* song with the super-funky beat. Many days, I can't get this one out of my head. "I'm gonna pop some tags; I only got twenty dollars in my pocket... this is fucking awesome!" How much can we save people? Better yet, how much can we save and then invest in order to build up some wealth so we are calm in our birthday suits? One's skin is much more comfortable when there isn't pressure to force a sale or come across as needing the money from this sale. Snakeskins and snake oil originate from snakes in a tree, warning us of the peril or urging us to make the mistakes we may face by making the wrong choices in life. One day at a time, one careful choice at a time, we can serve others and succeed. What if we were to sell only products that help others? The world would be better. I'm sure you can think of a few examples of these products that help people. Sell them. And get off the drugs.

If I see a hand-written sign that says *"Pressure Washing, I Do Great Work,"* the chances are excellent that I will call the number on this sign instead of the one with the flashy advertising. The reason is that this person put effort into the sign instead of money. This person *needs* the money and doesn't have money for flashy. The person with the fancy sign *wants* the money and has the money, and may even be less likely to give some of it to the person who needs the money.

When we spend more money on the flash, we end up short on the cash. If we put effort into ourselves and our work, it becomes less like work. Imagine how much a person starting his own company must care in order to create a sustainable business. A sustainable business stays in business. This person or business is more likely to pay attention to the little details and to ensure the client becomes a referral. A sustainable business needs money, not wastes money.

This lone person, pressure washing things for people in a caring and kind manner, is setting the tone for a business that can succeed. This, in turn, is setting the tone for an entire community. Be the person helping to create a better community through your caring and your service.

Flash or Cash? Which would you rather be known for? Showing care and attention to detail is outstanding for building good habits in business. But if the care and detail seem contrived and almost fake in order to try to "wow" the customer, then it becomes a gimmick at that point. The businesses that make things super flashy and more luxurious, like the salesperson that tries to look like a luxury business, are the most likely ones to fail. When things get tight, these fancy rockstar clothes may even become a source of depression for the person who focuses on them. When will the Oscars become more about great talent and great stories than it is about the red carpet? Flying carpets are more magic. Winning with magic is tragic. Luring others to like you isn't how to get sales. Proving to others that you are able to work hard and care about them is the most sustainable way forward.

People make mistakes (I just raised my hand.) Young people are more likely to buy fancy clothing and furniture than older ones. My worry (based on everyday observations in the world of service) is that purchasing flashy things is becoming an addiction to be reckoned with as our internet age races forward. Sex, drugs, and rock & roll are fun things to say and experience; however, these are the façade to the life we are building. Trying to lure others to love us by how we dress is a fishing trip where the big one gets away. Next time you watch an advertisement, take notes on it. Make the pros and cons list. Make a satisfying or frustrating list. Try to decide if the product being advertised is a need or a want. Try to determine whether the product being advertised is trying to promote sex, drugs or the life of the famous. Do this same exercise for a month while watching ads. Is it possible that advertisements are similar to the guy who wrote the book about eating at McDonald's every day? He ended up feeling sick. We are consuming something that isn't good for us every day when we stare at the screens. We are getting sick as a result of our addictions to the life of the rockstar. Be who you are. You can be a rockstar without being a rock.

Be You - Let's unpack this a little further. Remember Saturday Night Live's sketch about Stuart Smalley (Al Franken's character) when he affirmed to himself in the mirror, "I'm good enough, I'm smart enough, and doggone it, people like me!" Self-help does actually start with self-talk. We are a caricature of how we see ourselves. We project to the outside world an image of ourselves that we want them to see. When we do "dress up" as adults, we are crying out for something. Are you still a kid in need of something? What is it that you want? What do you really need? When do you feel at your best and most satisfied with your life? Now, think about how you feel when you are being served. Now, think about how you feel when you serve others. It's a circle of service we are seeking. Let's make each other feel good and make ourselves feel good by making each other feel good. Doggone it, you are good enough. Doggone it, people like you.

Dress The Part - My feeling is that we can focus on being the chameleon when it comes to saving money. Granted, some professions are sticklers about the dress code, but we are in sales. Our goal is to fit in with those we are serving, so we are just part of the scenery rather than the main entrée. By becoming part of the scenery of our everyday community, we then are at our most vital point to be able to affect real change.

By keeping how we are dressed from being a smoke screen or talking point for others, we are showing our genuine desire to serve others and will stand to gain the most vital advantage when it comes to turning the service into a sale. If we are genuinely always selling ourselves, then why are we also trying to sell our clothes, our cars, and our purchasing choices to others?

Yes, we each have our own "brand" and style because we are how we see ourselves, but it seems we are taking personal purchases too far as a society. The expectations from others that we should show how flush with money we are in order to then lure others into buying our wares isn't sustainable. The opportunity cost of using our money to consume too much is the prize that allows us financial independence. Saving and investing *today* will change our futures. Overspending today will decrease the chances that our sales efforts will result in high-end success. Should you wait to invest? Only if you are at ground zero and have absolutely no funds. But the investment into your moods and mindset will pay huge dividends even when there is no money to your name. I've been there. Stay positive, for sure.

Opportunity cost is when we continue to pay a power bill to an electric company so they can invest our money and work to get all the money. Why people? Why not invest your own money and own our power? There is a simple example here of how those who believe they have everything figured out and are so clever with their money are the least likely people to see the importance of saving money on the power bill. "No, I'm good," they say at the door, or "Not interested," they retort while closing the door.

The Buyer's Mind - So, let's get this straight and paraphrase the flippant answer at the door we hear from Mr. Buyer...*You are either* (a) 'good' at spending continually inflating money on something that you need, essentially renting your power until you die, and allowing *The Man* you have said multiple times that *you hate* to take your money and invest it at percentages of return double what you can get because you're just a rockstar in the world spending the money with wild abandon, the way you like to do everything, or, you are (b) 'not interested' in saving your own money from this day forward, owning your own power, and investing the savings into the future you are trying to build for a family that you have worked a lifetime to create for yourselves, thus, 'not interested' in keeping the college money for your kids, and 'not interested' in paying off the power bill before you're on a fixed income, and ultimately 'not interested' in (c) allowing our beautiful sunshine (that we only get to see on the vacation) pay for the vacation we can't afford to take because *the man* trained us to stay in line, raise our hand, speak when spoken to, and just pay the bill! Ahh, hell no. We would rather pay the inflating bill and not go on vacation. Really?

People, if I didn't care about you and your futures and your money, I wouldn't write a book about the absurdities we endure by getting into a groove of spending and overspending. You can and shall break free of the oppression. Your voice is being muted. Your will to think for yourself is being curtailed. Your desire to overcome the unfairness that has been devised to hold your free will at bay can and will be fixed by your mind. You have the brain. You care. You have the excellent sense to save the dollars and cents. You don't need someone else to do it for you. The days of having someone else nurse you and wipe your behind are over. You can move beyond this moment where the doldrums are slowly baking your will to live while you lie in a rowboat at sea. You are better than you think. You can work hard and smile while you are doing so. You can kick some severe walls down and remove the obstacles holding you back. You can, and you will be the 'you' that came forth from the womb to be. Let us be; let us all be—no more hide-and-seek people. Don't hide from the actual math of your lives. All you all come free. Let us think. Let us rise out of this muted mind. Let us be.

When we are kind, caring, and informed, it is possible to infect others.

Is Caring Contagious? We all sense that yawns and the sound of trickling water making us urinate are contagious, so how about caring? If we can infect each other with caring through our actions, like smiling at a stranger, then we can achieve life's most difficult tasks. Caring is the critical ingredient for a business to cultivate. Do you smile at others and say hello during the day? Thank you, Maya Angelo.

Caring and kindness are tantamount to creating sustainable businesses. If we put our money into name-brand clothing and fancy watches and shoes, what does that inherently say about our security? And we do know what it says about the rapid descent of our check balance.

Insecurity is also contagious and is often caused by bullying, lack of money, and lack of a proper purpose. When a group of classmates or coworkers laugh at someone, business deteriorates alongside morale. Those who are clear on purpose (the why) in their lives stand a more substantial chance of enduring and resisting the judgmental world we share. Thus, these are those most likely to have the confidence needed to be strong in the face of judging. When we show confidence in our demeanor because we know we are kind and caring people, the service we are able to give is solid. Why do we do what we do? Why do we work for these people? Why do we represent this product? Be clear on your why, and make the goals that will row your boat back to shore.

We hear people say to dress for success. The rockstar actually became talented at something, yet they also had to put on a show. The outfit is part of the show in showbusiness. It is dumb to overspend on clothing because it holds back our ability to achieve our true potential. Overspending isn't a story that plays well with sales.

When we can offer solutions for people who are shopping for a particular value, why do we want to give them more than we can afford? Businesses and people fail when they overspend. Be sensible, and be you.

Yes, Joan Jette would suggest we put another dime in the jukebox, baby... but I may be less likely to spend the dime and more likely to stop on a dime. *"I love to Serve and Sell; invest another dime in your future today..."* Let's stop throwing it all away, our love, our love (thank you, Brothers Gibb...), and start throwing around some love.

Best Side Story: We went to Missouri over the past week and went to the Johnson County Fair. One of the trainees on the team was fresh to America, by way of South America and Dubai, from his home country of Tajikistan. His sister had taught him how to speak English before he came. So, within ten days of arriving in America, this energized and optimistic sales trainee (son of a Christian pastor) made a powerful impact on the Midwest and all of us who were running the Solar panel booth for the community event. His exuberance and appreciation for his opportunity in this country were amazingly infectious and energized the whole team. "How are you guys doing?" he would say to every passerby. "You all have a great day," he would call out as they walked away. Within just a few days, he had a complete command of how to set appointments for solar panels to replace the power bill. Nate decided he would have no fear and overcame objections with great skill. He speaks four languages and told us he was so fortunate to have a chance to be in this free country, free to talk to his fellow Americans, and free to learn and grow. If you ever have a chance to see the immigrant experience up close and personally, you will see why America is great. You will also see how we can heal every wound that exists in this country. The appointments he set could yield him $4000-8000 in just the first ten days in America. His sister made $250,000 in her first full year after graduating college from a Christian school in Kirkland, WA. She used all her money to get her brother into America. We are all so fortunate. Seriously, do you realize what is possible in your life? You can do and achieve anything you can dream up. I will help if I am able. Please feel free to reach out for ideas; you never know what is possible.

And if you are in sales, throw caution to the wind, and remember, our problems are first-world problems. Nate's father, Rustam, the Christian pastor, was run down by a car less than two years ago and died at the age of 52. Life can be lethal as a Christian in a Muslim country. May he rest in peace, and let's all say a prayer for those who will carry on his name and legacy. Thank you, Farah and Nate, for all you have done for your fellow Americans and our families. Service is real people; we must help lift each other. And thank you for coming to America. Nate doesn't look like a rockstar, but he sure performs like one (but he is a black belt, thanks to his father's help.) And his brother, Daniel, is a rockstar. He is still in Russia and won 2nd place in The Voice of Russia a few years back. Common denominators? You do the math, but I would say tenacity, a desire to work hard, and a little prayer from time to time have had something to do with all this success. Effort, hard work, a strong father and mother, and a solid foundation will lift us.

This is America. We can make America greater each day. And we have always been excellent. We are growing, and we will always find a better and more harmonious way forward. Every day, in every way, we get better and better and better (thanks, Coach McGrath.)

Chapter 16

Here to Serve, Avoid the Curve

Progression, the A,B,C's of Service (& Sales)

When my daughter was not yet old enough to say words, she would hum the exact notes of the A, B, and C's melody (*also, Bah Bah Blacksheep and Twinkle Twinkle Little Star, all the same song...*)

It was as if she were a small doll, pre-programmed with the tune already inside her. For me, this struck a few nerves of thought at the time. First, I wondered how she could do this already. How could a kid who has not yet been in the world for over a year be so pitch-perfect? We are kind of musicians (like a foodie, but with music) in my family. Mom had spent a ton of time with us when we were little, trying to get her six boys to all get on the same page for a song with harmony. She used to say that she had dreams of us being like the Osmonds or Jackson families. Repetition and discipline made us get better at singing together, but only a few of us also loved the dancing part that came with the whole show.

Enter the chameleon. When a team works together to create an elevated service result, the end user is in the driver's seat on how the product is made. By using the talents of everyone on the team and allowing each member of the team to add a creative genius that adds value to the product, the process of inventing better service is alive. The chameleon feels the mood and culture being set by the leadership, reads how to represent this product best, and also notices what the audience desires. The chameleon sets the tone in response to the tone sensed during the presentation.

If the clients' feelings are hardened, they may come across as non-receptive, and the chameleon will change the energy and help alter those receiving the information about the product. When the chameleon blends into a synergistic scene, in whatever setting that presents itself, there is *a becoming* that transpires. *All players need a becoming* during a sales and service transaction. The client is becoming softened and conditioned from the moment the meeting starts.

The chameleon (you salespeople) becomes the audience and the ambassador of a product, and in essence, an extension of the ownership that devised the strategic plan to provide the product to the audience all at once, thus braiding several elements together simultaneously. This is achieved by being authentic, by being one's self, and by being situationally aware of how the manner in which the presentation is being delivered and received is coming across to the audience. This is also achieved by the ability to fit in and blend with any environment. *A becoming* transpires to make the transition into each new sales habitat.

Becoming is at the heart of being able to be a superhero service agent. Why are you able to go from being an everyday person, full of ever-lessening frustrations and negativity, to a new reality where you become a chameleon? How does this transgression occur so that you are able to take on the qualities of the people and places you show up to serve?

Progression is the answer. In order to progress, learning must occur. In order to be effective in service (& sales), the heart must soften, and the mind must adapt to become one of growth and giving. When you are in front of a client, do you ask yourself, "How can I make sure this sale happens?" Most salespeople do, and it does make sense that this is the dominant mindset.

Pop the question: When someone proposes marriage to another person, what are they suggesting? In essence, they are making a case to another person that life will be better for both of us if we get married. More profoundly, the proposal suggests we will both live a more synergistic life if we (our product and the buyer) are together. In other words, if we progress from being unmarried to a state of being married, we will be better off in the long run.

What would happen if you were to ask, "Why does this person need my product, and how can I help them see how it will make a positive impact on their life?" Also, the question, "How does what I know have the capacity to serve this client in a way that will change their life for the good?"

It is one thing to learn to love music in life. Sometimes, it takes an innate talent, maybe luck, maybe something more divine, but a predisposition for music is helpful, as with my daughter. But to become really great as a performer, one must have the capacity for learning, growth, and progression. Practice and putting in the reps on the musical instrument is the precursor to being an accomplished musician. So, with a bit of aptitude for learning and a predisposition for the capacity to understand the notes (by being a music chameleon), we can take our propensity to progress to the next level. When these people prepare themselves for a world starved for great music, they are nearly ready to perform. And once this person starts to perform for an audience, they realize that a little bit of dance will make the whole endeavor a little more endearing and entertaining.

So how did Michal Jackson become the one in the group of children to be the first to seize this understanding, then apply it to his trade and become the superstar? All the other children had massive talent as well, and they all put in the work. However, Michael's ability to progress beyond the others involved a work ethic, some excellent guidance from those in his sphere, and an ultimate desire to be the best at service. He truly wanted to serve his audience something they weren't used to seeing. He wanted to keep trying, keep learning, and keep pushing until the things he was capable of doing were so unique and memorable that the people he was serving couldn't wait for the next time he performed. Everyone would talk about his performances. The audience was in awe of his abilities. When Michael showed us his skills, not only with music but with dancing, he showed us a progression to a place where he created synergy from thin air. He knew that if he affected the hearts of people, thus becoming part of their lives, he could achieve anything.

We, as chameleons, are adapting and changing the world. We are taking all the learning we have cobbled together and are building upon it.

Adaptession is the word that comes to mind (add to the dictionary; it's all good.) Definition: *Through adapting to our environment, one progresses beyond today and creates a new future for ourselves and others, thus becoming the next step in the quest to thrive and survive.* **A** becomes **B**; a **C**hild becomes an instrument; **D**evelopment happens, and **E**verything is possible. **F**abric becomes clothing. **G**ood becomes great. **H**ubris becomes humble. **I** become we. **J**aunt becomes a journey, and so on... We progress, and we adapt. We become an instrument of Adaptation.

If we try to skip steps or take shortcuts, then the whole alphabet of progression isn't available to us, which leaves us lacking the vocabulary to make the right moves to become Michael Jackson. (Let's focus on the positives of his journey and legacy.) But when we push our capacity to move to a new level and are inventive, we create the vocabulary, and our efforts take us and our audience to the moon (walk.) Is it enough to know the music and not include the dance? Of course. But when one folds in one's unique talents, which were, by some stroke of luck, inherent to the being and soul found within, one becomes the person one was born to be and is ready to serve others.

Do you ever wake up with a burning desire to learn more and serve more? I do. It wasn't adapted this way, but through an *adaptation* mindset and the desire to move beyond my knowledge base and talents of today, I am on the way to becoming better each day. This growth mindset is equivalent to experiencing your *becoming*. Yes, a becoming is like an awakening, but more profound and more nourishing to the soul. Becoming is the holy grail of finding one's true self.

Here to Serve, Avoid the Curve – There is a natural curve to life, to the progression. We are born, we learn 90% of what our brain needs to move forward by the age of five, and then we go live life. If we are correctly steeped in service, it becomes a fantastic life. There is a point at which people feel like slowing back down again. This is the curve. It is a bell curve that lives typically follow. We rise, then we slow it down. Why do we need to slow it down? Do we want our bodies and minds to stagnate? I would like to know my great-grandchildren. With the proper mindset and a bit of luck, I can be on a course to do this. Please understand how critical it is to your sales (and life) development to keep serving others. Stay away from the frustrations and negatives and seek satisfaction and positives.

I want to sing with you, a choir of voices working to better our lives. And for me, a little dancing would be even better. Let's dance (thank you, David Bowie.)

Listen to some music and get yourselves fired up.

Chapter 17

Drowning in Kool-Aid

Drink their Kool-Aid first

How does it happen when we end up representing the wrong products and spending our lives doing work that doesn't make us feel well?

Many people do love their jobs, just like many love their president or their schoolteachers. But what about all those who despise the work they do and the people in charge and want to find a way to get on to something else? This is the gut checkpoint of the book. Is what you do for a living making you feel good about yourself, or the opposite?

You've likely heard the phrase that someone has drunk the Kool-Aid of their business. Enter Jonestown, Guyana. Blind devotion to a company, political party, or leader is rampant today. People have been letting the autonomous thinking they learned when building their foundations be muted. We were taught as children to go to work for a company in our chosen field and stick with it until we retire. This is how the financial successes people have been seeking are often achieved. Just like the adage about boiling a frog, if you put it in the water when it is cold and slowly turn up the heat, it doesn't realize it is being killed and is gradually lulled to sleep. My dad used to say, "One day, you're gonna wake up dead and realize you missed the chance to live." He always had some good quips, and I still wonder if they were funny on purpose or by accident.

Opportunity Costs - So, we spend our days making choices. If we choose to watch the daily news, and it makes us depressed, we have decided to drink the Kool-Aid. When we are drunk on something that makes us feel bad, then we are missing our chance to live the way we want to live. I realized the other day that my eighty-four-year-old mother, a person who reads all the time, didn't yet know what the word opportunity cost meant. And how would she have if she hadn't read a book about economics? Sometimes, we assume people know all the things we know, so we aren't sure how they will arrive at the decisions they make. I'm sure you've said to yourself or others before, "I never would have... (fill in the blanks,") or, "he should have...(fill in the blanks.) Our mind is filled with information that has been stacked upon our foundation, so we usually know what we would do in a given situation. However, until we are faced with the same problem someone else is facing; there is no way to know what we will do because our past and experiences are unique to us. Everyone is different.

So how would someone allow themselves to get into a situation where they enable Jim Jones to control their mind? "I never would have allowed that to happen," (again, are you sure you wouldn't have allowed it?) someone may say about the Jonestown situation. We are social creatures, which means we are easily influenced to let the status quo of our lives speak loudly to us each day.

Back to the question for the ten and under kids. If you had the choice to either rent a video game every day, and the price went up every year for the rest of your lives or instead own the video game and use it for no additional cost above what was paid for the game every day for the rest of our lives, which would you choose?

The obvious answer, even to the youngins... But the vast majority of us are frogs in the water and accept the water that is slowly warming to boil us. Or are we? Some want to pay the power bill rent and keep moving, make more money, and let the monopoly game beat them. Some beat the game by becoming the owner of the things we need, like the Hotel or the restaurant when we are on a trip. Those are items, one-offs, to rent. But the everyday items we rent will suck the money from us into the enormous power vacuum in the sky.

It doesn't matter how much money we throw at the power bill; it will keep going up, and we will lose the game. Same story, different day. Some folks do stop and ask themselves, "What can I do to stop the madness? You're damned if you do and damned if you don't!" Then, they stay in the water as it warms around them.

Are we being fed some Kool-Aid on a mammoth scale and just going along with it? Will each of us at some point realize that we can stop the madness and make different choices? I would have gotten the heck out of Dodge if I saw the Kool-Aid choice being presented to me in Jonestown. But maybe I would have been just lulled to sleep and drank it. That is what I believe is happening with power bills, insurance companies, and perhaps even higher education. These items are, for the most part, something we think we need in order to compete in the marketplace. Isn't it possible that we can buck the trends and come up with solutions that keep money in our own pockets rather than lining the pockets of others? If letting the sun pay your power bill can allow you the freedom to deposit money into a college account for the kids or your retirement account, what is stopping you? There is one solution. And there are dozens more solutions every month if we look closer at our spending habits and all our habits. In the chapter before, the flesh was described, and the ideal world vs. your current world. The flesh, or cash needed to buy our needs and wants, is available to those who are willing to change their mindset. All it takes is a decision at the moment, writing down what you say you want for your own life, and then following your construction plans for how to achieve the life you desire.

When we drink the Kool-Aid of someone else's business idea, we had better be sure that the business is placing service to others at the forefront. Because businesses aren't people and instead focus on the almighty flesh (dollar) alone, the willingness to think like a person becomes muted. Businesses are fighting the urge to be more robotic. They may state that jobs need to be cut, the service team needs to be refocused, or hours of operation need to be constricted. All these are in the name of the dollar, not in the name of service.

Drink the Kool-Aid that is good for you. If it makes you drunk, should you be drinking it? I know some of you would say yes, of course. But are you saying yes because you *really* think you should drink the spiked Kool-Aid, or maybe you are more likely to drown out the background noise of your life and the unhappiness you are allowing yourself to associate with the life you were gifted?

How can you find the right Kool-Aid for your life? One that will make you happy with yourself each day and satisfied with your choices. Where is the Kool-Aid that brings joy to others and doesn't make them drunk or dead?

Look no further than converting your mindset to service. Serve those around you. Don't feel locked into serving your company that doesn't have the same moral compass as you. Stand up for yourself and overcome the oppressing system that has guided your sheep mentality toward the squeeze chutes where the final moment is fatal. Use your life for good. Embrace all the positives in life, every moment, with each smile you deliver to another. Kindness is free. Love can be free. Love can also stifle us into doing things that don't align with excellent service. A selfish love toward another who is also selfish isn't the type of love we seek. Instead, selfless love toward other selves who are likely like us and need help is the goal we aspire to.

We sometimes feel we are just another brick in the wall (thank you, Pink Floyd...), but the Show Must Go On. The lyrics are, "There must be some mistake; I didn't mean to let them take away my soul. Am I too old? Is it too late? Where has the feeling gone? Will I remember the songs...The show must go on!"

And then, we take stock of the moment, and with a new strength and hope for our capacity to grow, we go on.

All of the songs earlier in the album are bathing in the present. A present that is informed only by a past. Our prism, those qualities and foundational moments that worked like a river through a canyon to define us, allow our mind to be present and respond to the future. If we fill the river with positives, get through the rapids, and ultimately survive until now, we can take comfort in our ability to overcome adversity. We can drink better Kool-Aid and leave the bad stuff for others. Then we can help others see how this isn't good Kool-Aid because look at all those sick and dying people over there...What is the opportunity cost of having a negative mindset or working in a hostile service environment? Let's go, people. We can be the hope. And yes, we can go on. *The Show Must Go On...*

Chapter 18

Teaching it to A Child
Without the Duck Noises

Service is a way of life. Sales are also the same, a way forward from a young age. Not only is it contagious, but it is also infectious. When a child catches the sales bug, it may be a life-long condition.

Now, some kids sell baseball cards, and they will become natural salespeople someday. The lemonade stand is also a great starting point. The parents try to set up the kids for success at the sales stand. My brother shined shoes for the neighbors when he was a kid. I was one to dive into the ponds on golf courses, then clean and sell the balls back to the golfers in egg cartons the next day. We would get $9/dozen and broke one of Mom's washing machines to get them clean. People did stuff in the eighties that isn't quite as doable today, which is the case with each new generation.

Knowing how to hustle will always be a great talent in the early days of a person's sales training. Yes, the desire to sell is ingrained from a young age and can be a form of early addiction when it comes right down to it. It comes to some naturally, and to others, it takes more effort.

Service mindset takes a little longer to take hold as an arrow in the quiver of the sales hunter, but this arrow is the most lethal. When I was around ten, my Dad and uncle would take me duck hunting. I learned how to shoot flying objects by practicing with clay pigeons. They made sure I would give about a two-inch lead from the aiming bb to the front of the flying object, then pull the trigger. Just the opposite of perspective drawings, the farther away the object in the distance is, the more the distance is growing more significant from the distant target. So, a two-inch lead is more likely to be a 3-foot lead in front of the duck. But besides the mechanics of shooting things in the distance, I liked doing the duck call. If the ducks plan a landing near the duck blind (shooting spot), we would get a shot at the duck. I would always think I was the reason that the ducks landed near us. Mostly, the adults did the shooting, but I wanted to be of service, so I called in ducks and ran out to retrieve the dead duck from where it landed. My Dad and uncle loved my intensity and were always complimentary of the work I would do on the duck hunt.

When we are young, adults make funny sounds at us to get a reaction. Duck noises are an ingrained humor instigator for children. When a person imitates a Donald Duck voice and says words, kids love it. Kids can be taught almost anything much quicker than adults are able to learn. So why do adults have such a difficult time relating to new concepts? If a kid learns to speak Spanish at home and English at school before the age of 10 or learns how to hunt early in life, there is an excellent chance that this kid will be bilingual and know how to hunt for a lifetime. It is the same concept as the "Teach kids to fish, and they can eat for a lifetime."

Teach a kid to serve... So wouldn't it also be true that if we teach a kid to serve, they can *serve* and most likely *eat* for a lifetime? This kid who can serve has a much stronger chance of becoming integral to any team, whether it be a sales team, sports team, a band, or the military. It's no accident that our police and firefighters are sworn to protect and serve. The doctors take the Hippocratic Oath as a reminder not to harm and uphold specific ethical standards.

Service Above Sales Oath (The SASO Principle) – I am proposing that salespeople be well served to lift the profession to a new level and initiate an SASO principle. In Rotary, the concept is called service above self. However, corporations aren't persons, and they can't operate like a service organization with a complete and honest desire to offer nothing but excellent service, so there can be no self in a corporation. Or can there be, and we just haven't seen the entirely excellent corporations yet? Corporations seem to err on the side of reducing their SOP (standard operating procedure) activities to serve the almighty dollar. The cold, complex world of "It's just business, don't take it personally..." is often devoid of allowing people and the families of those they serve to be at the heart of the decision-making processes. Thus layoffs. Thus, there is a failure to protect employees from dangerous chemicals. Therefore, many other practices prove that corporations are not the same as people.

If a choice by a corporation isn't best for the shareholder's dollars, then it is a decision that is hard to get past the board. And this is where the gut check for corporate officers needs to have a "come to Joseph" moment. What is this moment you speak of, Joseph?

What if corporations got better? Will the SASO Principle, that is, the *Hippocratic Oath of the Sales Profession*, require us to forfeit money for the good of the customers and the long-term oath to serve the customer, above all else? I predict that the coming decades will require corporations to embrace service at the top of all decision-making processes, or else they will fail. Safety is service to the customer and employees. It requires caring and kindness in order to serve others properly. So *Safety First* is **<u>Service First</u>**.

Suppose the answer to the SASO Principle question returns a "yes" in this "come to Joseph" moment. In that case, the board will choose that money shall be spent to further a more profound customer service solution, thus extending the long-range trust between the company and the customer and creating a safer place to work and buy products. This will reduce warranty claims and will increase trust among all stakeholders in the company's success. The shareholders also include the customers, their employees, and their families. No wonder Unions were invented. Maybe they could do a better job of ensuring work focuses on service, but the primary function of unions is to give the employees a unified voice. The SASO principle will provide all stakeholders with a better product and a more honest environment to build trust between the corporation, the employees, and the clients.

Theodore Parker once stated, "The arc of the moral universe is long, but it bends toward justice." Justice can be defined as (1) *the exercise of authority in vindication of right by assigning reward or punishment,* (2) *the quality of being fair and just, moral soundness and conformity to truth.* In the building, when something is justified, it is straight or made suitable. Corporations are punished by bad reviews when they treat the customer or the employee poorly. When we build with straight timber, we have a level structure. Be straight with each other. When things are bent, they are unjust. So, if the arc of service is long, it is best if it were never an arc, to begin with; instead, it is consistently solid, always straight, and a complete, unwaveringly truthful disclosure. This is how excellent service is achieved. The whole truth, and nothing but the truth, is the bedrock of service (& sales.) If this isn't possible for your sales organization or corporation or you as a person, then it is time to go back to the drawing board. Retool your thinking and focus on service above sales. We, as people and corporations serving one another in our communities, need to be morally sound and just. When we serve one another, we are kind to one another. The phrase, "It's not beneficial to the shareholders..." is no longer an excuse to give bad service. Go into almost any bank nowadays. They have all the money and provide the worst service. It is actually laughable how poor the service has gotten in the place with all the money.

People, we have a choice. We don't have to use banks that act like this. This goliath of an organization doesn't deserve to be trusted with our money if they cannot care about us. I mean it, take a closer look, people. Like Ross Perot once said, "There is a giant sucking sound..." of our money leaving our bank accounts. We are forced to pay interest to play the game. We are forced to pay fees to pay the gamer. The gamer is gaming us in their game of Monopoly, and we are all losing. What is the golden rule? He, with all the gold, makes the rules. Same as this, "Cash is King!" Which means the banks are our kings. We are the serfs. We shall not be afforded a situation that allows us to take control back of our funds unless we can see the truth of what is happening.

An example here. When a monopoly power company sets the prices, they are bound by two factors. One factor for their accounting is that they cannot charge us more than it costs them to generate our power on a day-to-day basis because they are a regulated monopoly. On one hand, this is comforting. So they must have our best interest at heart. Oh yeah, corporations usually are devoid of a heart because they aren't actually people. So, the little-known fact (dirty little secret) is that they can raise their rates for capital improvements, which are a whole different category in the accounting world. Meaning they have a free rein to reign freely.

Their capital improvements are major renewable energy expenditures, battery and solar farms, wind farms, renewable energy research and development, fixing decrepit power lines, and upgrading existing facilities. There is no limit to the amount of expenditure that power companies will need to pursue to strengthen the sick and weakened grid in the coming decades. If they ask for more funds, then they can usually have the funds, and then the rates can rise due to this side of the accounting system. This is how the monopoly gets to make huge profits—quite an excellent trick to suck the cash from our pockets further and totally legal.

Question: What will you be paying for power in 5 years? How about 15 years? There is no way you can know. This is completely and utterly outside your control, except for the fact that it is not outside your control at all if you end up owning your power. So own it. Really, why not?

Sorry for getting so caught up on this power bill thing, but this is my public service announcement book for the nation and even the world. Let's all wake up and own power like it is the human right that it really is to us.

Back to the kids... Because even kids understand this stuff...hear me out below.

So why do we wait until high school to teach languages or to teach financial planning? Why are children able to see simple math without judgment, but adults aren't? We show kids the math for Solar instead of paying rent on a rising power bill, and they get it. Try it, show your kid.

As a kid, there is no history of having made a poor decision to pay a higher price for the past decade or more, so there is no need for the child to invest in rationalizing a different answer to the math we teach them like there is for the homeowners; no reason to save face for having decided the more expensive route and wasting money for years.

Pride goes before the poor financial decision. Husbands and wives are willing to tell themselves and an energy specialist that, "We have already done the math, and it doesn't work for our family." I explained this before, but again, it should be said that pulling the wool over each other's eyes instead of doing real math is a disservice to one another, and the same is true of lying. Why lie about stuff when we can tell the truth and save money by doing so? Kids, should we lie or tell the truth? Corporations, should we lie or tell the truth?

Why are we teaching the kids one thing and then doing another when we get old and run companies that are supposed to do nothing but make money while telling the truth? Is it because lying helps increase the bottom line? If it does, and you are OK with that, then it is time for you to switch professions, get out of politics, resign your leadership, or find a different way to serve others. There are helpful ways to serve others, but lying in order to make money isn't OK. I have tried it, and it does not work for sure. I stopped stretching the truth to fit my needs. I hope you will do the same.

When we approach the sharing of information as a service to the buyer, there is more likely to be a receptiveness to learning what we are showing people. When we instead position previous decisions of the buyers as an oversight on the part of the buyer (renting power instead of owning, who knew we could own?) rather than making them feel guilty for not having thought of the correct math answers themselves, we are more likely to get a receptive buyer. Give them an out, and make them feel clever.

Let's not make the buyer feel bad for not figuring out the shortcomings of their purchase choices previously. The added guilt piled upon the buyer will manifest itself in wanting to hide under a rock or get away from the person serving (or pointing out the shortcomings in the thought processes said buyer used to arrive at the previously erroneous purchase decisions), the embarrassing correct math. Tread carefully in this discussion, and don't make them feel stupid.

The best way to serve others is to share new information with them and help them understand better what wasn't known before. It is essential to make sure the buyer understands one concept before moving on to the next. Methodically, the teaching service then results in sales.

Think of some of the things that you have sold in the past. Did you use service and teaching to help enlighten your customers? How could we expand upon this and really take service to the next level? Corporations, it is time to step up and own good service. Tell the truth.

The following questions are a great way to flush out how your organization could get more robust. Where are you missing opportunities to serve others? How could sales decisions be framed as service opportunities instead? Who among your sales team is a superstar service agent? What can we learn from this person and their perspective? How would reorganizing the mindset of the entire team help strengthen sales? How would we best dialogue about ways to increase service?

I would love to help with this process and hear from you your ideas. I am able to help facilitate the brainstorming needed to help move the brain of your organization to a different place.

Hunting for sales is very fun. And sometimes, duck noises are fun. Learn to hunt (& serve), and you will feed yourself for a lifetime.

With customer-centric service, _Your Exploding Sales Will Empower Customers Authentically, Now_ (YES WE CAN!) This means the reviews will be excellent, and referrals shall go up quickly for all stakeholders in the service (&sales) experience.

How many times have you had absolutely fantastic service experiences in the past year? This is a dying art. Be curious about others. Imagine how you could help them with their buying experience and their excellent life experiences for the day. How can you make someone feel better today? How can you be the positive force in a process and create a memorable experience because it is positive rather than negative? How can you inspire customers to give a good review?

When hunting, we have to re-think things and aim out in front of the duck. Pre-think your sales strategies and be ready to service those who are your sales targets. It takes practice and requires a slow and steady hand in order to have a good aim.

Again, most negative reviews are harmful because they weigh ten times more, as shown in an earlier chapter. Let's fill the cheerful bowl with chocolate chip cookie dough; again, this time, grab some milk, too and take the time to cook the cookie perfectly. Let's have a fantastic dessert made from butter, sugar, egg, flour, chocolate and vanilla, and truly enjoy our days together. You deserve a treat... serve someone.

Chapter 19

Programs for People Like You

In your Situation, which is what?

I n sales, the condition of one's reasoning for either "purchasing, postponing, or punting" is often referred to as _disposition._ The disposition of a sale is a description of the person's mindset at a given time in relation to other events and details of the life they are currently experiencing. People are either open to learning about something new and considering a new outcome for their life choices, or they are not interested in learning something new at the time. Inside this last sentence, many characteristics are waiting to be discovered by the interrogator (you). The buyer that says "not interested' is equal to instead saying "not curious." People often are so overwhelmed by the current situation they face that they can't then imagine piling any new information into the calculus of their lives. "I don't have the bandwidth right now" could also be what they are saying when they say, "not interested."

Why is this the perfect time for the buyer? If it isn't the ideal time, what would be a better time? Be able to give suggestions for the listener (buyer) of better times in the coming days, weeks, months...

What are we trying to learn about the person's disposition? If there were to be a perfect time to learn about why our product would solve some of your problems, "What would be the best time to learn about what we are showing people like you?" could be a better question.

'People like you...' works. *"We have programs for people like you, that is, people who are looking to save money in their home budget and are looking for a way to avoid postponing having control over their finances."* This sentence is a good one to memorize so that the chances of your product or service being bundled with the person you are talking to grow exponentially. People need your product, so how are you able to show this is true and that you end up still having the solutions that will help your life pivot? Talking about the other people in the neighborhood or community who are just like them, as a collective voice of reason, is a great way to get buy-in from your customer who hasn't yet bought in.

Solar helps those who help themselves. Saving helps those who help themselves. Change happens for those who help themselves. These concepts are all true.

When programs are designed for people like you, the subtext then is that people have already been taking advantage of the program, and they are happy with their results and happy they have been made aware of a solution that can help them.

One of the most potent ways to arrange a proposal to learn something new and to have the proposal enjoy some level of success is by seeking to understand a person's disposition. *Talk with them first, prior to starting to propose anything.* Underline or highlight this last sentence. Conversations are a collaborative effort. Work to listen more than you talk when learning. The ears and eyes are the recorder and camera for the collaborative media and results you intend to create. Your collaborations are the content of your life. It takes patience to learn and to teach.

If we listen closely to the 'hot points' we learn from the customer while we are first meeting them, then we are more likely to address these 'hot points' in our proposal and hold their fears at bay. Another way to say this is to listen closely to what the customer is telling you because their words and objections will be the words and objections that your "program" will be addressing in order to serve and help this person. This customer will tell you how to serve them and what will be needed from your program in order to work for them. In essence, they will tell you how to sell them.

While this is a straightforward concept, it is likely one of the most challenging parts of sales to master. A sales pitch is often just that. A pitch across the plate that is hopefully one that will connect with the buyer's bat. What if you were pitching to a batter who told you, "If I could only have this program you are pitching be thrown slow and right about knee height, I could hit a home run when the bases are already loaded so my team could win." As an opposing team member and a pitcher, you would do something drastically different than give the batter what he wants because you would like your team to win.

However, if you were conversely a person paying a power bill that rises by 15% yearly for the next two years (hello California) as the State Legislature has already voted for, but you don't have enough money to pay the new high bills because you already have month-to-month income that is barely enough to live on, you would hope that the "program" being pitched by the service agent would be able to provide a never increasing power bill, that eventually will be paid off. This is the world of Solar sales and service in the 21st century. The client is asking for no more increases, and the sales-person is able to provide just that with the program being pitched.

We love to hit the ball and see it go far. Nobody wants a bunch of fancy pitches that are hard to hit. People want things that are predictable and things they can control. When things are out of control, like ever-increasing rent for power, it makes them feel anxious and unsure. When people can see an end to their problem (paid off power bill), they are pleased in the moment and more likely to decide to start changing their habits today.

What is your disposition? How could you characterize the things that are missing in your life, and how do you think these voids can be filled?

This desire to fill the voids is part of what drives the entire economy forward. So, if there is a void in the service industry, I desire to help everyone take notice of these shortcomings we see in the marketplace and put an end to them. What voids in the market are you experiencing? Do you have ideas for how to address these? Feel free to email me at josephdevine@mail.com with any short comments (500 words is enough) so that people like me can help you think about how to apply better thoughts to your situation. Together, maybe we can make a difference.

The biggest _problem_ we all face every day is poor service. The _solution_ is creating products and series of service habits and programs that end up helping us **_to help one another_** more thoughtfully and kindly, without simply being further controlled by the "powers that be..."

Who among those reading this book is worn out by people, politicians, media outlets, corporations and advertisements that only highlight the problem? Where are the thinkers? Where are solutions better than those we have heard thus far? Where is the creativity that people are inventing every day going?

The Cancel Culture is quashing the solutions. A negative mindset is being farmed and flourishing among our positive efforts. Groups and organizations are working to quell anything that threatens the life of the products and ideas that rise from us. Negative people on the News Outlets seem to desire a world where pointing out the problem is enough, and creating fear in those who have solutions to solve the issues is the norm.

People have grown fearful of telling their truth and afraid of asking the right questions. Some politicians seem to be scared to say, "America is already great, so why can't we keep America great and make it even better for the liberty and justice of all?" Fear of retribution from bullies is a real thing. People don't want to be in the crosshairs of those controlling negativity. People have become afraid and thus have quietly become complicit to the fearmonger's strategies.

If we learn to lose all fear, ask to be part of the teams seeking solutions, and then work for a life that is bound to help those who most need the help, our friends and posterity, America and the world are growing positivity by the bushel. We plant the seeds of positivity every day, and we become stewards of positive growth and solutions. The positive mindset solutions will show up at the ports, such as barges filled with wheat that are delivered by oceans to the masses around the world. What if it were this simple? We can find the solutions.

Here is a new idea that may be squashed by those who stand to lose if they don't control it. There may be a power amplifier on the way to the world. Rather than explaining it here, know this is something of significant consequence that would change the world immediately. If it were to work, then people could hypothetically go to their basement in the morning and ride the exercise bike to create enough power to fill their battery bank for the day's power needs.

Suppose someone has invented an amplifier that multiplies power by ten times. In that case, a power company wants to control it rather than having everyday people get to make money off or be able to serve themselves from the idea.

This reality happens every day in the world. Great ideas get bought up and shelved so that the powers that be (monopolies, governments, etc.) can continue to control the subject being governed and depleted of fortunes. Taxation and inflation thus rise, but those who don't retain control over the things in their lives they need are adversely affected.

So, are there programs for people like you? What is your current situation? Please write down the things we discuss in the exercises listed above, or grab a piece of paper with a fresh mind today and start becoming a scribe for the life you desire to create for yourself. We can do amazing things when we work together. It takes only one voice and one idea to become then the contagion that will help feed more positivity to the world we live in.

Quincy Jones and his friends showed us all how our voices, our art, and our ideas have made change possible. We Are The World became one of the top ten singles of all time. Those who participated tapped into the heartstrings of over 20 million people willing to purchase the single so that the idea could fund some real change. *"We are the world, we are the children, we are the ones who make a brighter day, so let's start giving..."*

Your art, your work, your words, and your daily choices and behaviors are the keys to all that is good. We fail sometimes. But when we do, we must learn to grow and get better. Today is the best place to start, and then keep building upon this positivity from today forward. Amen.

Mom always said, "If you can't say or do something nice, then don't say or do anything at all." And conversely, "If you can say or do something nice, be the one to do it, start today." And help others see the power of this mindset and the power of their choices and habits. They can be changed, and you, too, can grow. All of us, you and me, can grow and become better than we were yesterday.

Chapter 20

What's Your Problem?

Quickly Becoming the Solution

One Valentine's Day a few years back, it was the first time I had been in a town different from my wife's on this lover's day. We had decided weeks earlier that it would be better to earn money that day and not cut short the business trip, and so we were both in agreement to sacrifice the celebration of love to facilitate higher earnings this year.

This is always a tough call. On the one hand, one wants to do something great for the significant other, and on the other hand, if more money were available, something even greater could occur and be afforded for the pair. Money. By talking about it earlier, we were able to be at peace with our decision. Was it the right decision? I'm not sure, but at least we decided, and time will tell.

Had we not made that decision, I would have kept the same pre-assumed notion that nobody would want to buy Solar on Valentine's Day. I was sure that people wouldn't be answering the knocks at the door that day, and it would have been all a waste and it maybe would have been better to be with the wife because love is mainly best demonstrated through time with the other, not through things and presents.

So, on this Valentine's Day, I decided to knock on doors at about 1:30 p.m. I at least wanted to keep working until 5:45 or so but vowed not to interrupt the dinner hour. A half-hour into my journey, I met a woman who opened the door of her double-wide. And after one sentence to her, she exclaimed she had been waiting for someone who knew how to help her to come along. Her problem was that she had been told by three previous Solar guys that she couldn't make it work for her because of her double-wide.

I was invited into the home and proceeded to show her in about fifteen minutes how it would work for her, but the other Solar guys didn't know how to do it. Her simple problem was easily solved by knowledge, and within a few minutes, she decided to call her twin sister, who also had a double-wide, and told her that Solar was doable for her, too. Within under three hours, by about 5:30 pm, we had sold two systems on a day that I had assumed no sale would happen. My partner and I split the commission for the day, and both made about $13,000 in those four hours. The system was installed within a week, and the payout for the commission was in hand by March 1.

Every person has a problem and knows their reasoning for why a product wouldn't be correct for them. The challenge to find a solution is sometimes days, weeks, or months in the making. Other times, the solution is simple and can be worked out in a matter of minutes. One never knows when the next client will be the simple solution to address, but when it happens, it can smash all previous assumptions to pieces.

Service (& Sales) is about putting in the reps. Repeating a prescribed regimen of cold-calling or follow-up will be rewarding. The seeds we plant today are going to be harvested. So, the more seeds we grow, the better the harvest. The most amazing sales-people have a striking capacity to work diligently and pursue a tenacious desire to serve others. This doesn't necessarily come naturally to people. It is achieved through effort and retaining joy as a guiding principle in one's journey to excellence. There is no perfect solution for the client, but there are excellent choices for them. The more you know, the better prepared you are to solve the problem.

How will you become one of those at the top of your game and ensure you have solutions for your most challenging clients? Repetition and tenacity, these traits will be among the answers you find for this problem.

Follow-Up - Having an excellent solution for your follow-up habits is another problem to solve. I have tried many different ways of trapping the information about leads, from excellent CRM applications to hand-written lists, to Excel spreadsheets, to constant lead-generation behaviors. The more I dig into the best behaviors and practices, the more I realize that duplication in schedules is an essential factor in providing great prospecting results.

- Have a predictable CRM system that integrates with the schedule. All phone numbers, emails, and addresses, complete with notes and dispositions, are here.
- Once something is scheduled, schedule it again in one or two more places. I would like to have meetings that will make me money in three areas. (1) My business CRM schedule, (2) my schedule, (3) written on a week-at-a-glance schedule by hand to recap things, either on Sunday night or by Monday midday. If this means I need to wake up early Monday AM to get my brain focused, then so be it.

- If items are changed or postponed in one place, move forward only after having rescheduled in all three areas.
- Set meetings that make you money every two hours. Start at 11 am, and then continue scheduling them for every two hours. If you need to fill in additional meetings, then in the 1 hour between the last two sessions of the day, start here and move backward from there. So if eight meetings to make you money were to happen in one day, the last parts of the schedule to fill in would be the 2 pm and the noon. Set things up so you don't inadvertently run behind as the day progresses.
- Be diligent about pre-communicating to the client about the meetings, and don't worry if they feel like postponing. It is better to communicate and risk a cancellation than not to have communicated. The more times we touch the client, the better. If they try to cancel or postpone, take this with a grain of salt and encourage the client to understand that we want to do this meeting at a time when they feel comfortable and calm so it can be a productive discussion. Keep pushing forward; they are likely to continue if you go to continue. Even if it is months later, keep moving forward. There is no hurry and, for sure, no pressure here, people. Our product is worth the wait. And they will remember you for your kindness and understanding.

Life in sales is about solving problems. The more we ask questions, the more we will discover the problem the client is facing. Is there a problem you have been facing in your life that needs to be addressed? Have you been saving too little money for the last many years? Have you been overspending without thinking about it? Have you failed to put away any money for retirement or education for the kids? Have you been too busy working to make ends meet to make the time for proper planning? Have you written a budget for you and the family and then reconciled the actual expenditures to the budget you set? Have you been trying to accelerate the pace at which you spend on your perfect living situation without taking notice of how it is further strapping you and thus depleting your savings? Is today more critical than tomorrow in your world?

What will we be able to do to address making changes to our lives? There are many problems, and time is scarce. How will we change course and finally take control of our own financial life? Sales are driven by service. Service to ourselves drives our capacity to serve others.

There is a time and place for solutions to our many problems. Today, one can change how today is. And if it works today, we can make it work tomorrow. And if it works tomorrow, we can envision a way forward for a week. A few weeks later, we lived a month with our new habits. And the seasons pass while we grow and learn to earn. A year will bring a fantastic change, and two years will bring more change. Five years from now, you can have a unique savings plan in place with emergency funds in place and a strategy to build a decade-long habit that will grow our legacy, make us calmer, and ensure we leave our affairs in order for those we love.

It starts now. Please, each of you, think of how to serve yourself and others. Be a part of the future we are hoping to build. A calm, kind, and growing person is here inside of us. Let's share this person with the world.

We were born penniless and will have died and left this world with no more than we brought into the world. Others may continue our excellent work, and that happens. But it all starts with good work. How will you be remembered? What problems will you solve? Most of us have been steeped in a world of materialism. It stands to reason that we selfishly have put money in front of the well-being of others. We can break the mold, and solutions can start with you today.

The problem? Sadness, searching for love, and no meaningful experience with adulthood. How did Prince turn the sadness on its head and make us want to dance? In 1984, the year I graduated high school, my best friend and I went to Honolulu for graduation to mourn the loss of high school and celebrate the future. And the drinking age was eighteen, so a little freedom would help us solve our penned-up problems. In the basement of a club, after midnight, we discovered our first Midori Kamikaze drinks and *When Doves Cry*. We would never be the same. We found ways to move and dance that had never occurred to us that night. Growth happens. There is always a solution; we must see it.

Decades later, I still remember that feeling of dancing and being with my friend. We had a blast, and these actions were part of my journey. However, it is a progression to continue the process of learning. I stopped drinking about nine years later and figured out all the good things start happening at a higher rate when one keeps the mind clean and ready for the next challenge or opportunity. The Kamikaze was the only part of that side story above that didn't make me feel good the next day. So why do it? I was eighteen, who knows. But I grew. When we are trying to solve problems, we are at our best when we use our minds and bodies to the fullest extent possible. Listen to the doves cry, hear the wind through the trees, and smile at the times behind; let's go live in the now... *really live and serve our way forward.*

The Prince song spoke to my primal desires and helped solve my problem. The Valentine's Day sacrifice did pay good dividends, but I still regret working that day. Money isn't the answer, but it does help to have some when solving problems, and I know this is true.

It is all a balancing act. Just err on the side of love and service and minimize the tendency to hold money up on a pedestal. Nobody will remember your money; they will remember you and your desire to serve others. Take it from here, Prince... *"Can you, my darling, picture this?"*

Chapter 21

Learning Financial Tendencies

To Better Serve Your Solution

Some leverage their money and pay interest, and some pay cash and earn more interest themselves on the interest they didn't have to pay. Knowing which type of person is the target of the service (& sale) you intend to help is an important starting point to understand how best to help the person and to know how to become a "have" instead of a 'have-not'... And what about you? How have your money habits unfolded?

Everyone is raised with a different set of priorities and philosophies when it comes to finances. Some are taught how to save and invest money, and others are not. The value of hard work is often taught, which is near the top of the list for how to build wealth. However, the time value of money is less usually taught and is most often not considered when people are doing their budget math.

Prior to 2008, banks dominated the world of corporate credit, underwriting debt and either holding it on their balance sheets or selling it to others. Then, when 2008 brought about the credit crisis, things started to change. My home-building business and my real estate values plummeted at this point. The private lenders, not affected by the same regulations as banks, stepped in to change the balance of lending toward private lending. In 2004, 60% of the loans that banks arranged and placed in the public debt markets were worth less than $250 million, according to S&P Global. By 2020, that proportion had fallen to below 10%. The private lenders have since moved to much larger loans. In a 2022 Reuters article, Johnathan Guilford and Neil Unmack wrote about how, in 2010, the average company borrowing from Ares, one of the largest private credit firms, had an EBITDA (Earnings Before Interest, Taxes, Depreciation, and Amortization) of $37 million. By 2021, the typical borrower's EBITDA was $162 million. This is a 437% increase in just 11 years.

Private lending is overtaking the banking sector due to less regulation. So, when lending is less regulated, risk increases. We as a country are in a precarious position when one looks at these truths. Yes, 2008 was an eye-opener and adversely affected nearly all of us. But those few that still had the cash became kings. Cash is king, as surveyed in Chapter 18, is the concept that has given powers away from the rule-regulated banks over to the world of less rules, private lending.

With each new iteration of how to bypass the rules, the passing decades bring more and more money to those who have all the money and less to those who are being controlled by those who have all the money.

So the concept that I present in this book, that service to one another is our most robust way to combat the funneling of our money away from those of us who don't have enough money to those who have all the money, is potentially a last-ditch effort to help each other understand and know what is at stake.

If we stay with the status quo, where power companies take all of our money, even though we can make our power and don't need it any longer, we are just postponing the inevitable truth. All our nest eggs are being fried, boiled, and otherwise converted to mayonnaise to slather on the bread of those who have all the money. Slowly but surely, it is evident that the rules keep changing for those with all the money, thus leeching the nutrients from the soil of our own lives.

There is a changing of guard for each generation. With each passing decade and looming financial meltdown, the system of institutions that make and enforce the rules and regulations seems to be more embroiled in either a shell game or collaboration in making it easier for the haves to pull more wealth from the accounts of the have-nots.

Service is a way for us all to help each other notice what is happening and hopefully take action. When service to those needing the most significant help becomes a more substantial part of the corporate decision-making process, the need to maximize the bottom line may take a slight hit, thus slowing revenue growth. Still, the positive result will become more people who have a fighting chance to benefit and gain by being a customer of our product. It will leave some money on the table for the customer.

The constant tendency to maximize corporate profits through seeking higher prices, selling more volume and reducing the level of service through reduction of payrolls and overhead is loading more responsibility onto the governments, which are then forced to take care of the companies that get forced out through bankruptcy and the families that can't afford life in the inflationary higher unemployment world it all creates.

If we treat our budgets like those who know the time value of money do, we would all be spending less and investing more. I had to learn these lessons the hard way. Although I was taught in the few years after deciding to forego a college degree about how the money I make could and should be able to work for me and enjoy growth through compound interest, my long-term memory for the lesson started to fail first. My income began to rise, and I began to feel more invincible. Once I started making and being in charge of more significant sums of money, hubris would set in, which then caused me to rely more on leverage and interest and less on saving. "I have the money to do it my way, and darn it, I will do just that..." Has this been your mindset?

The isolated stories of our finances all have pitfalls and successes to mention and learn from, but the larger long-term picture seems to be more challenging to keep in the front of our minds. This has been my experience, at least.

When will the primary schools start to include more lessons about how to gain through compound interest? When will the budget balance be a full year of study? When will the downside of being a renter of products versus being the owner be apparent to children, so will the aspirations for saving and ownership help offset the materialism that has risen to become a driving force of our economies, thus depleting savings?

I'm hopeful that we can each do a better job of buying less and serving more. When we serve ourselves first, thus saving for the rainy-day fund, we have the power to help one another get out of the quagmire of debt we have created for ourselves and ultimately stand on more solid ground. The foundation and bones chapter at the outset of the book needs to be revisited at all points of our lives. Not just at the beginning.

We have the power to change our habits today. Elton John and Bernie Taupin sum it up in *Someone Saved My Life Tonight*... "I'm just a pawn outplayed by the dominating queen... You're a butterfly, and butterflies are free to fly, fly away, high away, bye, bye... I would have walked head-on into the deep end of the river, clinging

to your stocks and bonds, paying your H.P. demands forever..."
These lyrics remind me of being indentured servants; we are
walking head-on into the deep end of the river, paying our ever-
rising interests and power bills, and using our money to rent a position in life.

We need to own it. We need to help each other get through this
dilemma. We need to be of service to one another and not of
service to our debts. Bye-bye to the old mindset. Jump at the
chance to change life now. Use the money you make wisely
because there will be rainy days, and we will want to be able to get
through each storm until the next sunny day arrives. Let's become
a choir that we all then help to get on the same page and ultimately
preach to ourselves. By pointing out the pitfalls that I have experienced myself firsthand, I am hopeful that I can help make a difference in your lives and help you avoid making the same mistakes.

We will increase our sales and saving habits through service to
others. Let's empathize with each other, become chameleons, and
help each other master this same mood for change. The slow but
sure change we create each day will help our species outlive this
moment. Peaceful days are ahead.

Please take notice of the little things, such as a piece of fruit and
toast in the morning and a nice long walk with our spouse. We can
enjoy the moment without spending and help others do the same.

Chapter 22

The Ultimate Service

Hospital Advocacy...You are What Matters

Yo. What if a single book could awaken an entire country into realizing there can be hundreds of thousands of dollars transferred back into their lives, helping them to be much better situated to increase their net worth over the coming decades? What would billions of dollars back into the pockets of every day struggling homeowners do for the overall economy?

These are the questions that have compelled me to include so many examples about a single liability that faces nearly all of us, that is, the power bill.

What if the same book were to show people how to increase the productivity of their soon-to-be-required renewable energy solar panel systems and decrease the rate of degradation of the panels themselves, thus slowing the need to recycle panels in the coming century and consuming less of the world's valuable resources in the production of said panels?

Luckily, this book does both. If you haven't yet figured out how key it is to your financial future to make your power from the sun, then mentioning it again here is worthwhile for sure. Please look into it and see how your family can put away an enormous nest egg.

If the book hadn't mentioned any of these ways to save hundreds of thousands of dollars on power, the hope is that we explore the power of hospitality in our lives.

When we build wealth for ourselves and our families, we are better suited to serve others. Many of us have had a time in our lives when we needed to be present for an ailing family member. Even with my brain surgery last year, I came to realize how important it was to have my wife present to talk with doctors and caretakers about my condition. When we are sick, we do need help. Take a moment to thank those in your life who have helped you past these tenuous times, those who were there for you. Their hospitality has become a critical part of who you have become as a person.

They say when the going gets tough, the tough get going. But sometimes the going is more than we can handle, and if we don't have help, we may not make it through the situation, no matter how tough we believe we are or have been in the past. This was especially true for me.

I was never one to worry about going to the doctor to get things checked out. Having grown up around sick and dying horses, I knew how resilient the body can be. "This too shall pass" is the phrase that rides shotgun with me wherever I go. But when I contracted Valley Fever, all of that was turned upside down. I learned later that, when left untreated, 85% of people who contract the fungus will die in the first year, and the next 15% will die in the second year. Without drugs, this fungus will overtake a human or animal, and the fungus will win the fight to survive.

So when five different doctors failed to diagnose my situation correctly, my wife took to the internet late at night and figured out what I likely had contracted. Have you ever had anyone save your life? I have. I was up to twenty-two hours per day of sleep and still was sure I could sleep it off. I didn't realize I was being eaten alive by a fungus, but I indeed was. The blood tests came back positive, and treatment started eight months after I had first contracted the ailment. As the summer progressed, things became more dire for me and culminated in spinal meningitis, causing pressure in the brain and the ultimate brain surgery to solve.

"This too shall pass..."

Sometimes, it feels as though our will to survive and thrive is a miracle. There are many seemingly miraculous moments in most people's lives. But when we come out the other side of the brush-with-death moments, it adds to the fierce urgency of now.

When we give the kind of care to one another that we would receive if our lives were endangered, we stop thinking about money and instead hold the lives and health of those we love and care for above all. What if we were to do this same thing before things get dire?

Are you financially sick yet keep going through life without the hospital advocacy needed to help you through the situation? We have become a culture that puts helping and serving others behind the importance of money. We are less likely to ask for help when we need it because we have been raised with this "pull yourself up by the bootstraps" mentality.

If we instead were to celebrate both the hard work and the service to others at the same time, the health of our country and selves would be fertilized and thrive. Who is the advocate for your financial future? I skipped this part in the first fifty years of my life and am retooling to incorporate a sustainable way forward. Luckily, I love work and know that it will be the one saving grace for my financial future. Having decided to place service at the front of the line of priorities in my life, I see how it is possible to satisfy all my debts and progress through the next forty to fifty years (God willing...), creating a healthier prognosis for many people around me and my posterity. At least I will die trying.

Having had the brush with death has focused my mind on how to make service the core component that will drive my success. Others have helped me to make it further down the road, and this is the time to pay it forward. How many people have helped you to achieve your livelihood? What if those people hadn't been there?

Hospital advocacy for those around us is a way of life and a winning mindset. There will be times when things are dire and when you know you didn't practice your own beliefs, so the hospital advocacy you hoped you could live by isn't doable. There may even be times when it feels like your life is a living hell, so how could you help others and serve others when things seem hopeless? Remember, if you find yourself walking through a personal hell, keep walking. Tenacity will propel you to the next moment. This too shall pass... and if it doesn't pass, and instead you pass, let's hope your spiritual dreams are realized and you become part of the better place you've dreamed was possible. No matter how dire the dilemma you face or have faced may seem, there is a positive way through it, and your ability to conquer adversity will help you become more robust in the process. Keep going. Help each other. Do things that make others feel good, and lose the bad habits.

No matter what pitfalls you have endured in the past, you matter. You are capable of massive growth, and you can and shall be part of the solution for us all. Take your lumps, and keep going. You have made a difference in the world from the day you were born. Let go of the negatives and work toward the dream of a day when you can help right any of the wrongs. Your hard work and your selfless mindset will help extract you from any predicament you find yourself in. McGiver, the situation, be inventive, and keep rollin'...

Forgiveness lies at the heart of those who desire personal and community growth. Let's do this thing.

Be the advocate for those who need you and for those you may have hurt in the past. They need you to keep trying and be there in the ring—service mindset. Serve. We all need you.

Chapter 23

When Does Money Matter?

Being Able To Massage A $100 Bill

When does money matter? If this question were to be asked thousands of years ago, money would likely be less critical than it is today. The day we are born, money has no value to us. When we are dying or nearly dead, or in fact dead, money doesn't amount to anything in our minds. It is the time in between those two events that seem to dominate our fixation on money. In the first five years, cash is barely a concern. And in the last five years, the value of money to older people has started to lose its significance.

Older people seem to come upon a realization that when their life passes, the money they have acquired will be distributed to those in their will. And if there isn't anything left to distribute, they understand that somehow everyone will be alright. Just the same as hundreds of generations that came before them, the bucket of money remaining once divided among heirs reduces the concentration of wealth because several different people then hold the wealth that one person had previously held. The heirs either build upon the money or they squander it.

As time goes on, the sad truth is that a few at the very top tend to end up having the majority of the money.

So when you're there wondering how to make ends meet, and you are living paycheck to paycheck, you are one of two people in America doing the same thing. Half of your neighbors are in the same boat.

So imagine these two boats loading up at the pier with people and heading off to a new country filled with the promise of a more equitable distribution of wealth. One of the boats (50% of the people) would be the boat headed toward the country where the chances are 4 out of 100 that you be part of the households earning over $122,000 per year, and the other boat is filled with those who will undoubtedly earn over $122,000 per household per year.

The tickets to get on the boat headed toward certain income and questionable income are different prices. The particular income boat costs one year's wages to board. The questionable income boat ticket is free. Which boat would you be able to board right now? Which boat would you want to board? If a lending institution were at the dock and were giving twenty-five-year loans at an 8% rate with no money down for the whole $122,000, would you buy a ticket to board the specific income boat? The payment would be $1000 per month for the boat that brought you toward a certain income. The rates of inflation have historically been around 5% for both the places the boats were headed. How do you make the correct decision? The boat is leaving the harbor, and there are no more boats planned to sail at the time of the decision.

People come to America regardless of which boat they get on. They are able to start with nothing and then rely on their hard work and luck to deliver them from one income bracket to another. But how do they do it? If one of the boats were going to America, a proven democracy based on laws that have lasted nearly 250 years, and the other was headed toward the newly established country of Certain Wealth, run by an autocratic government that had absolute power, which place would you go?

As shown above, many people are willing to pay interest in the future to have the promise of a certain income. This theory breaks down when one thinks of the many factors that interrupt the concept of a certain income. Take home ownership and student loans as examples. The interest payment may, in fact, work out to secure a future with better gains. But what if it doesn't? What if what we think is certain only takes into account the facts that we know right now? This concept is why the actuary sciences are needed for corporations and individuals with high wealth. The future conditions and probabilities that may affect one's decisions today need to be estimated in order to make better plans for the future.

The reason corporations and those with wealth want to secure as much cash as possible is so that when the going gets tough, the cash they have on hand will be able to swoop in and pick the meat from the bones of those who have less security and no money to solve their problems. In the great recession of 2008, many over-leveraged banks and individuals got stung really severely, and many realized the catastrophic failures of their business models.

My home building organization was one of the near-failures at this time due to being leveraged with many properties that all dropped in value at the same time. There wasn't enough cash on hand to satisfy the banks that were asking for their short-term construction loans to be paid off. If the loans were to be extended for a matter of years, the prices would have risen, and the eventually rebounding real estate market that happened four to five years later would have solved the problem because equity would have grown and satisfied the loan-to-value requirements. However, when prices are lower than the amount loaned because values sink by over 40%, there is no equity. Selling at a low time means losses. And when one doesn't have the cash to satisfy the losses, failure is subsequent.

All lessons are learned in some way. Sometimes, the hard way is the only lesson that head-strong deciders can get the message. The main components that keep us from having the cash to be in charge of our financial health are overspending and interest.

As a person in sales, you may make good money, sometimes great money. That's all good for the time when things are rolling strong, but what happens at the lulls and when the headwinds are too strong for the leveraged budget? The only solution is to _not over-leverage the budget._

Be able to afford to pay cash for the things you buy. If you do end up having to pay interest for an investment or home, make sure you have enough equity (over 40-50%?) to withstand the fallen market conditions when they are to happen. What I have learned is that these conditions will occur. It's not a matter of 'if' they will happen but 'when' they will happen. Re-read this paragraph repeatedly.

Your ability to survive and flourish depends on your financial health. Systems, programs, and even institutions may and probably will be stressed to the limit at some point in your life. The interdependence of the financial world is undeniable. When one sector sees significant challenges, almost all the sectors (real estate, stocks, bonds, etc.) can experience the same challenges.

When, at the age of 56, my health took a turn for the worse, and death was narrowly escaped, all of these points became clearer to me. There was no savings to fall back on due to past debts in my construction business. There was no way for me to pay my bills when I was sleeping over twenty hours daily. When I couldn't pay my life insurance, it was canceled. There was no support system nor an emergency fund to rely upon. The State had to help me with medical and doctors' bills. After my first brain surgery and I started healing, the insurance companies all decided my Valley Fever diagnosis would not allow me to get life insurance any longer. Their competent actuaries agreed that my situation wasn't one they could take a risk on. In essence, the new lifelong fungus that would be with me would almost certainly result in an early death from complications that would result from my condition. If the insurance companies don't take a risk on your situation, then you know it must be dire. Gone undiagnosed, 85% of those with Valley Fever will die in the first year. The other 15% will die in the second year. This fungus kills everything.

It seems like insurance companies are almost always willing to take our money, but I was able to find a reason why they won't any longer. Stay away from dust storms in the Southwest, for sure. They may have a fungus that will infect your system, and the doctors in the Northwest may not figure out why you are sick until it is too late. I will be on medicine for the rest of my life, and this sickness has demolished my ability to predict the future challenges I will face from contracting Valley Fever... Now I have been enrolled in a study at the NIH, only 180 other people in the last 10 years have become part of the study, to try to find reasons why Valley Fever affects different people differently, pre-existing tendencies, and other reasons why my case was so severe. I'm number 181... They will pull blood, prod and push me around every year for the foreseeable future, freeze and feed my blood to keep it alive for decades and centuries even, and eventually , hopefully, learn how to make this less likely on others in the future. Human lab rat, or living organ donor, either way, it's the least I can do for having America and the State of Washington help save my life. Modern medicine... Bring it, Pink Floyd...*The show must go on!*

I have kids and many families depending on me to survive and thrive, so it is time to push forward again. If Walt Disney can survive and thrive after bankruptcy, why can't anyone else do the same? And I didn't declare bankruptcy because I would rather pay everyone back who is still owed money. If that seems counterintuitive to you, I understand because we have been conditioned to let others carry us forward when we cannot bring ourselves.

But we have also been conditioned to take more significant risks than we should. I took big risks and had failures, and I want to try to make them right with each passing *big* year. Hopefully, I will live long enough to do so. I do believe I am more potent than the fungus that kills everyone in its path. Modern medicine has been made possible by tons of intelligent people who are outsmarting ailments. Everyone is standing on the shoulders of those who have served them up to this point. Service and sales are the way forward. They are the only way forward for me. Thank God for everyone who has helped me get to where I am today. I wish I could have learned the gravity of poor financial planning more quickly before experiencing financial failures and medical setbacks. Still, now I know and am working with what I know to help myself and others try to see the reality of our situations. We are here to serve one another. With knowledge and kindness, we can join together and do so. We can all do better. I intend to do better and survive to experience the Disney rebound...

When one is able to massage a hundred-dollar bill, make it last longer, and make it work for you, then one's relationship with money is on the rebound and is healthy.

I will serve others to help them become more financially secure and will die trying.

Chapter 24

Lifelong Product

Service, The Final Frontier!

Service is a lifelong endeavor that brings us from birth to death. We are either honing the craft of service to others, or we are honing the craft of serving ourselves. The latter will take us far but will not take us anywhere we want to go. Service to others should be the cornerstone of our lives. When we give, we get. When we forgive, we can forget. When we want what is best for others, we make the right decisions. When we want what is best for ourselves, we often make mistakes.

After having read many different books about service myself earlier in my career, I was still not savvy enough to avoid major pitfalls. Having flawless integrity is the final frontier. When we act in only a truthful manner at all times, we will become the most sought-after product. How many of you can say you have never cut a corner on integrity? Have you ever paid cash for something you needed and then didn't include it on your taxes so you could make more money? I have yet to meet any adult past the age of thirty that can answer no to that question.

If you are willing to cheat the system just a little, then aren't you potentially willing to cheat your customers just a little bit too? What else are you willing to cheat about? Will you stretch the rules just a touch to get what you want or need? Is it possible to leave this mindset behind and work from this day forward on honing the honest service everyone desires and deserves?

This problem in our America of today is one we will need to solve in order to have the type of service it takes to help one another arrive at better solutions. Politicians are going to need to stop cheating. Business owners are going to need to stop cheating. Is cheating fraud? Tax fraud occurs when one cheats on a tax return in an attempt to avoid paying the entire tax obligation. So, if one has paid cash to someone else and then didn't claim it on the tax return, that person would be guilty of tax fraud. Have you ever done this? Have you ever worked with someone under the table?

Tax fraud includes claiming false deductions, claiming personal expenses as business expenses, using a false Social Security number, and not reporting income. Have you ever done any of these?

Think long and hard about your answers, and ask yourself if there is a better way forward. Just because you may have gotten away with it in the past doesn't mean you should move past today trying to do a fraudulent event again. Stopping is possible. Just the same way people stop drinking, smoking, or cheating on a significant other, all untoward activities are able to be stopped.

In order to serve others most honestly and openly, without fear of disseminating lies in order to make the sale happen, one must use an extreme mindset of the most steadfast integrity and be willing to forgo the sale in order to best serve the client's long-term well-being.

Another quick green energy example: <u>If a company knows that a Solar Panel will last longer and be more efficient throughout the year by being cleaned regularly, then is it fraudulent to say, "No need for more maintenance on these panels; they basically take care of themselves, and it rains quite a lot here, so they perform better after the rain." Right inside the sentence is an admission that the panels work better when they are clean. So, I am worried that this double-talk only hurts the customer and the entire industry as a whole. And if an entire sector of the green economy has been passing on half-truths to the customers, are these solar companies saddling themselves with additional unneeded risk for claims in the future? Of course they are..</u>

Time will tell how this all plays out. It took nearly ten years after Ford's Model T production line had churned out thousands of cars without windshield wipers for them to offer glass cleaners right off the production line finally. Why did it take so long? How many people died in the process because they couldn't see where they were going?

In the Solar Panel example, how many clients have had sub-par production for many years because no education was provided to them about the increase in output and slowing of degradation that occurs when panels remain clean most of the time? Does anyone owe for the past negligent information? If the company learns that production increases and degradation is slowed by cleaning but fails to allow the team to talk about these facts, is there a cover-up happening that will haunt them later?

Again, time will tell how this all plays out. My sense that we can better serve one another by sharing the truth seems solid to me. Again, this was one of the main driving forces that allowed me to develop a service-first mindset to create this book. I do hope others in all sales industries will take service to a level that it has not yet been taken.

CNN Heroes: An All-Star Tribute is a television special created by CNN to honor individuals who make extraordinary contributions to humanitarian aid and make a difference in the lives of the beneficiaries through the great works displayed by these individuals.

I believe it would be just as powerful to create a show that highlights the *ACKNOWLEDGE Awards* (Amazing Customer Kindness Network Offering Workable License to Embrace Delivering Great Empathy) as a way to inspire companies and individuals to celebrate giving excellent service, above all else.

If it costs the bottom line to do so, then let's do so. In previous chapters, I mentioned that I was not in the service industry for the awards. But with the suitable awards, maybe I would have been more motivated always to do the right thing, no matter what.

Even without such awards, it is a service to the greater good of all humanity to make our efforts fall in line with a higher spiritual commitment to each other. Everyone has a different reason for doing so, but we are brought down and become more depressed as a society when we see others only in it for themselves. When we see companies, politicians, and everyday people getting away with poor service, maybe because they are just not familiar with how to provide excellent service, it affects us. It adds a layer of depression to each of us when this is multiplied throughout an entire economy and world ecosystem. Not caring is equivalent to multiplying negativity in the world we share. And when the negativity multiplies, just like plastic floating in the ocean, there becomes a tipping point that we bring ourselves past. The plastic straw on the camel's back may not be far from us.

Let's invent the awards together to celebrate excellent service (not online, where only the negative comments seem to get the airtime.) Let's legitimize Great Service as a guiding principle to the health of the entire community and each of us. It starts here, with us today.

How can I help you brainstorm ways forward? Please reach out if you want to help make vast and meaningful steps forward. Through collaborative efforts, it is doable. We can all pitch in and make it happen. Excellent service is like a potluck of ideas. We all can bring something to the table and then serve up a much better America and world than we currently are experiencing. I'm excited to be there with each of you to help make it happen.

How many of you watched Star Trek and were riveted by how it made you feel? At the time, it affected an entire generation. It helped us to think outside the box of our typical universe and imagine a final frontier. What if the frontier we imagine were to begin with the giving of ourselves to each other?

U2, let's pull us all together on this. *"See the stone set in your eyes, see the thorn twist in your side; I'll wait for you...With or without you...And you give yourself away... Nothing to win and Nothing left to lose..."* And this is a good thing. When I used to hear this song, I thought that maybe giving yourself away was a bad thing, and perhaps we were supposed to embrace being more selfish. But it was not correct, I now know.

Bono, who wrote "With Our Without You" with the other band members (Adam Clayton, Larry Mullen, Jr., and The Edge), could be interpreted to be about his relationship with himself. "I was at least two people: the person who is so responsible, protective and loyal, and the vagrant idler in me who just wants to run from responsibility." In his book, *U2 by U2*, he wrote, "I thought these tensions were going to destroy me, but actually, in truth, it is me. That tension, it turns out, is what makes me an artist."

For me, this song is the anthem for having a service mindset. When we give ourselves away, whether others appreciate it or not, we are coming closer to the relationship with our spiritual side and able to come to terms with the meaning of our own lives.

To serve is to give. To give is to elevate oneself and others toward a better plane of happiness. What more can we do to live a whole life than just give more to each other? Crank the U2 before the next chapter...

Chapter 25

We Are Actors

Becoming the best version of you...

When we are young, we tend to watch how adults act in order to learn the behaviors they use to navigate life. It is during these formative years that our way of being in the world starts to be defined. Some of you who have read this book feel that something may be wrong with you because you don't feel like joining groups or attending social gatherings. Or maybe you have felt so shy in a crowd that you have wanted to disappear and be somewhere else.

The feeling of being an introvert is often problematic for people to describe. On one hand, it feels abnormal to desire to be alone more than with other people. Or maybe you have thought it would hamper your success as you struggle to find who you are and then find a way to present yourself to the world.

While introverts may feel alone or want to be alone, there is likely a high likelihood that service (& sales) are the perfect fit for the lifestyle. It all may depend upon the mindset brought to everyday life, which is a compelling part of why I wanted to write this book.

When we survey some of the great humans of pop culture, introverts have learned and developed ways of coping with the desire to be away from people or find a livelihood that fits their tendencies.

Bill Gates has become one of those we revere as having sold the most products and having one of history's most potent effects on an entire generation's future of sales. As I use Microsoft Word to tap out words, I stand on the shoulders of an introvert. Of course, he was able to assemble a team and use his mind to lead and motivate others, but much of the work he has been doing has occurred in the solitude of his privacy. When the introvert comes out into the world, a new cloak of confidence is donned in the way of acting the part. Through repetition, by putting the cloak on and walking outside to brave the world, the introvert becomes a better actor.

J.K. Rowling once took a trip by herself to London. It was on this trip that she spawned Harry Potter as a concept, now one of the most-read book series of all time. Is she a salesperson, and is she serving others? Yes, of course. Her ideas have to make sense and appeal to a larger audience in order to gain traction and afford her an opportunity to keep doing what she loves to do, primarily by herself in a room at a computer. Again, we are all serving others in our way.

Warren Buffet, much like Bill Gates, is an inventor with a creative mindset. He has a flair for monetizing good service and understands the long-range power of becoming a good business. He has admittedly had a tough time connecting with people. By reading books like "How to Win Friends and Influence People," he overcame his solitary habits. He found ways to use his time alone to his benefit, thus becoming one of the most famous and wealthy investment experts of all time.

We are all selling and serving our own needs when we use an "adaptession@ mindset. We adapt; it does take some acting, and then we progress. It is our creativity and inventiveness that find a way to cut through the white noise of everyday life and put our God-given talents to the best use. The fears that pull us from having complete confidence are the very traits that help drive us past the feeling of danger experienced in groups or one-on-one presentations to allow then us to fight through the fear, thus using our creative capacity to enjoy *becoming* and *acting* like someone else who is less familiar to ourselves than our own perceived selves.

Yet, our perception of ourselves is part of what allows us to buy into being saddled with introversion as a crutch rather than a motivator. Once we become motivated to overcome introversion and push ourselves to new heights with our creativity, we will be well on the way.

What do actors do? They improvise and try things out. They also rehearse. There will be a way that best fits your style to get through the moments of fear that have held you back from attempting to become more excellent at acting your way through your introversion, but you will come through it with repetition and pursuit of adversity. As we showed in an earlier chapter, it is the adversity that we need in order to prove to ourselves that we can do it. When we put ourselves out there, we overcome, thus cementing in our minds that we can do it. We can do anything that is mathematically or physically possible. We may even be able to push the limits of math and physics to a new level. But we will need to sell it to a larger audience, somehow, at some point.

Meryl Streep and Audry Hepburn were both natural introverts. But they pushed themselves to overcome their tendencies and found the stage as a way to invent new characters and mannerisms that allowed them to shine on the big screen.

Michael Jordan, too, maybe a surprising introvert. His insecurities drove him to put more practice and hours into overcoming those traits holding him back than others had previously. Putting oneself in the face of adversity, daily, for hours, with a relentless tenacity is a recipe for overcoming obstacles.

Christina Aguilera, the outstanding singer of the song "Beautiful," is one of my all-time favorite introverts. *Every day is so wonderful, then suddenly it's hard to breathe, now and then I get insecure, from all the pain, I'm so ashamed...I am beautiful, no matter what they say, words can't bring me down... so don't you bring me down today."* If you haven't already listened to this song, take a listen right now, music break.

The power of music, acting, and inventing ourselves to motivate us and then move beyond what has been ourselves toward a new us is repeated every day around us by great introverts who find a way to put the past behind them and find a better path.

If you had your life to do over again, would you? It's a tricky question for many. Some would say they wish they could do this or that better, or wish they had tried harder, or wish they had been born into a less toxic situation for their lives, or wish they had more talent, or wish they had physical features that allowed them more confidence, but all these are a pretty apt description of a mindset many of us have shared. We all are broken and want to fix the things that make us feel "less-than" adequate. Hold that thought. Accept it, and hug the thought. It is OK, and we all understand each other's feelings. It is the next series of thoughts that come after these thoughts, the positive and solution-oriented thoughts that become the drivers of success. By wallowing in the "if only" of our lives, we are then stunting our growth. Like chrysalis, we do know how to metamorphosize our being. We can break out and move forward, becoming the butterfly we desire to be.

Reach out when you hear the voices of doubt creep in, and go to places unfamiliar. These places are calling you. The need for adversity is pulling on you like gravity. We need to be challenged, and we will rise to the challenge when we put in the time. By putting yourself out there and overcoming the tendency toward introversion, you will find a new you that you were not aware existed. When you add more layers of positivity, struggle, and success to your shy and worried frame, you become the most beautiful you can be.

Chapter 26

Teachers! Know Your Student!

Audience matters

When we are putting ourselves out there teaching others about our product, we are serving our audience. How many of you have watched the comedians who have become master improvisers by playing off the audience? This is a learned trait.

Think about Steve Martin, Martin Short, Whoopi Goldberg, Robin Williams, Chris Rock, Ellen Degeneres and so many others. How about the whole crew of Seinfeld, The Office, I Love Lucy, and Brooklyn 99? How do we feel after watching them for so many years? It's almost as if I start to smile just thinking of these people and the situations they portray. If I hear Will Ferrel has another movie out, I have to see it because he makes me laugh.

Most of these highly successful and complicated people have been able to use fun and self-deprecation as tools to propel themselves forward. Are they salespeople, and do they serve others? Yes, they are, and yes, they do.

The pursuit of excellence is learned by study and effort, and by being inventive, self-deprecating, able to keep it light, and by knowing one's audiences. We all yearn for humor in our days.

Prepare yourself. Read and watch others. See how others have dealt with difficult situations or demanding audiences, then allow your personality to start inventing ways forward that work for you. Is it essential to put yourself out there in front of new audiences every day? Yes. This is likely one of the most important things to ensure that it is happening. Go out in the world and put yourself out there. Then, your smiling comedic side will start to come out when you smile and have fun with the sales audience you are pursuing. Getting into the fun and funny mindset is equivalent to creating the smiling and lighter side of yourself that will allow you to serve those who you intend to serve.

Of all the traits I have seen in the most excellent salespeople, it is the ability to keep the moment professional and light at the same time. So, I try to emulate this my way. Yesterday, I was dealing with an attorney, trying to show him how to save money on his power bill by owning it instead of renting it. He was a tough audience, with a reasonably stoic demeanor during the presentation. At first, I tend to keep it relatively professional and informational when the audience (an attorney) is used to decades of professional settings and dealing with all types of characters and challenges. Plus, one always wonders about attorney-client privilege, I'm just saying. But as the conversation progresses, I can see some side glances and smirks toward his wife, and I am not sure what they mean, but I am guessing she does, after having spent years with the man.

"I sensed you were thinking something; sometimes I would love to be able to read the cartoon balloon above people's heads in moments like these," is all I could think to say because it popped into my mind, and I couldn't hold it back because I was starting to smile myself. I was trying to find the moment of fun, and in this particular moment, I did find it. He and his wife, in addition to the two gentlemen training with me, all laughed. This moment becomes a reset, thus lightening the mood. I watch a lot of comedies in order to have comments like these flood my mind. I want to have fun while I keep things professional and educational and moving forward. The critical moment is finding his smirk and then subtly building upon it with my smile and comment.

He ended up telling me what he was thinking, and his thoughts were much more genuine than I feel they would have been if I hadn't said something in response to his sideways smirk. But we take the cues from people we meet with, from our audience, and we work with what they give us.

While I'm certainly not an expert at this like the comedians we all know and love, I know I can get better at studying what they do and how they do it with each foray into comedy that I view.

What about John Mullaney and others like him who have built careers on the funnier moments and then have been able to both write about them and perform them? All of these people, with a ton of forethought and by focusing on the subject matter and a desire to serve a laugh to others, have become experts and commanding a winning emotional control over the mindset of the audiences. When we make others feel good, we are serving at our best.

The dopamine response is what we are trying to evoke in others. Chameleonatomy is about reading the audience and becoming like them. We want to allow our moods to arrive at a similar place and time so the comfort level is present in the moment, and the moment then becomes a positive memory. When we can do this with greater ease, through practice and through putting ourselves out there, we are on the way to becoming great at service to others.

Can the introvert work the crowd and lower the inhibitions of the audience? Yes, and this is where sales become effortless. "You've been a great audience tonight!" We all yearn to say these words and to be in the room when the words are said. The way they became a great audience is through the skill and ability to read the nuances of the audience in the first place. Maybe there is a heckler. So, get to know the heckler. Maybe there is a know-it-all, so find out what makes them feel good, and let them know how what they know makes a difference and then feels right to us all. Maybe there is a frowner, so try to find out why and help cheer them up. Perhaps they seem distant, so pull them closer. Maybe there is someone who can't stop laughing, and they are just letting go of all the pressure in their own life at the moment. Even the audience needs an audience, or a muse, to help them process what they are processing. Laughter is contagious, so keep smiling for sure as you serve others.

The teacher needs to understand the cues they are reading from the children in order to be able to teach them better and understand how to be most effective with them. Service to the children is what teachers do. The best teachers create the dopamine connection through their diligence in wanting to understand all the children they serve and are teaching.

In sales, knowing your audience is made possible through knowledge of the product you are serving and by understanding the problems the customer may be trying to solve. So, circling back to curiosity about the customer is step one. Asking questions about their day, their life, their past, and how the problems we all seem to share are vexing us all is a significant first step. Know the surroundings you are noticing at their home if you are in door-to-door sales. Avoid using cheesy comments, but rather genuine interest in the person.

A comment like, "Wow, I love your Tesla; what made you pick now to switch over to this brand?" may be an excellent question to start the conversation. If the lady who came to the door was wearing red lipstick, maybe avoid the cheesy comment, "Wow, I love red lipstick; my Mom always wears that color." But for some, this too may also work. The questions one asks of the customer should be questions that help the salesperson understand the problems they have faced or may be facing best, but without being too obvious. It's a dance.

In dating, it may be less effective to say, "Hey, I think you're hot, and I would like to get to know you better right now so we can take this opportunity to the next level and maybe determine the best next steps." Instead, the slower approach is always more advised.

Be situationally aware, understand your audience, have patience, and go out there and kill it.

"You've all been a great audience tonight!" There, I said it.

Chapter 27

Processing System

Fast Talkers, Speed Readers, and ADD

There was a time in my past when I spoke slower and less often. Having been one of the speech impediment people in the world unable to say the letter "r" was a condition I adapted to in my first nine years of talking. When I would say things like, "We're goin' to the "wodeo" "wight now," it would get a chuckle from anyone nearby. People and siblings would have fun repeating the things I would say, and slowly, I learned to talk less and listen more.

This may have been one of the blessings of my life that wouldn't make sense to me until decades later. Eventually, I learned how to say my "rs" by repeating the word purple and using words like it. What remained was a tendency to be a listener and, therefore, a learner.

In sales, although decades later, I am known to "fast-talk" when I assess the audience and feel they are learning at the same pace that I am talking, I remain highly aware of whether my words are going too fast for the lesson or sales spiel I am delivering. Usually, I warn the listeners to slow me down if anything I am conveying is going too quickly for them, but people won't often call themselves out for not being able to follow the words one conveys.

'The pencil and paper on a piece of paper help me to find the right pace for the learner. Often, having the audience or customer grab a pencil and paper and take notes on the things we are learning together is a great way to get the pace to follow the learner's synapse patterns.

With today's computer apps that aid in the process of sales, it seems there is a glossing-over that occurs in the learner's mind, like passively watching a television show, that appears to inhibit the ability for learning to occur.

In a Harvard-based Center on Media and Child Health at Boston Children's Hospital, pediatrician Michael Rich comments on the ever-changing digital landscape. "Boredom is the space in which creativity and imagination happen," he says. The seductive digital pursuits, gaming and social media tend to convert the brain to a "variable reward system, which is exactly what you get when you go to [a casino] and pull a lever on a slot machine, a sense of skill needed to improve."

So, as we show new concepts to people who have been conditioning their minds with an ever-increasing exposure to the screen, the screen itself may be inhibiting our ability to get the point across to the learner.

"We have to be flexible enough to evolve with the technology but choose how to use it right. Fire was a great discovery for cooking our food, but we had to learn that it could hurt and kill as well," Rich says.

The first part of this chapter points out the need to ensure that the person we are teaching the pros and cons of our product to is actually "picking up what we are putting down..." Many people will passively nod their heads when we are talking with them, and at the same time, they look at the screen in their hand or watch the television in the corner of the room.

Active listening is made more impactful when the pencil and paper come out. Everyone learns differently, but when we take out a pencil and paper and encourage those we are speaking with to do the same so we can compare the notes, we are requesting that we all agree to be in a learning mindset during the conversation.

My friends used to joke with each other that I was the only person they knew who would take notes while we talked in everyday conversations. While it barely happened ever (but might have happened a few times), the point they were making is that I was a student of everything, almost to a ridiculous point. But after a while, it seemed my brain was able to improve its ability to learn through my behavior. If I took notes while others were talking, I was more engaged. The teachers seemed to notice, too, which then increased the chances of getting an "A" in the class. But even more than this, my retention was more robust with each passing year.

I remember being intimidated by the concept of comprehension. Some of us are slow readers, which means we are searching for ways to increase the chances that what we read is understood and also remembered. In school, the regurgitation of information back to the test was drilled into me. The fear of not recognizing or comprehending what was being read drove me to try to get better at understanding *why* I was having difficulty comprehending what was being read.

When the teacher talks, I am able to read supporting information from a textbook, and then I take notes on all of this input, and I have the most excellent chance of understanding the concept being taught. Because of this, my propensity to make my sales pitch follow this same concept has evolved into one that relies very little on the computer and more so on the conversation, slowly, and the written notes we all take to achieve the learning together.

Fast-talkers has become a derogatory term, especially in the more rural areas. Wherever there is a slower pace of life, the speech patterns that are used also seem to slow down. This isn't so much because the rural people are any less educated, but instead, the culture in the small towns has been less apt to embrace the fast-paced language that has evolved in the bigger cities. So when I am serving (& selling) in a small town area, I consciously slow down my vocabulary to match the pace of the town.

Even when I am in a larger city, I still try to do the same thing. Slowing down the pace of the words coming out of the mouth and concentrating on whether everyone I am talking with is actually following my conversation becomes a critical part of the sales process for me to cue into how the audience is tracking. "Does that make sense," is a reset term I often use. "Any questions on what I have said so far" is another recap phrase.

It is essential to keep asking these reset questions so the paraphrasing process ends up being how we slow ourselves down when serving (& selling) others on a concept.

Having a little bit of a country drawl, like my childhood rodeo days, starts to happen when I am in the small towns. We seem to conform to those we speak with, which is all a part of the concept of chameleonatomy. When I was in Europe in the 1980s, I found myself using a lot of broken English when trying to communicate with Europeans. They probably would have understood me reasonably well if I hadn't done so, but somehow, for me, it seemed to help to try to conform to their way of talking when I was talking with them. There must be something to all of this.

Being aware of how fast we talk and even read is a big part of how quickly we learn things. Some rush through the reading of information and think they have learned it. But when we slow down to go over things again with these people, their minds start to ask more questions, and the "speed-readers" we are serving start to slow down to actually comprehend the subject matter we are conveying in our sales pitch.

When too many words are in our marketing materials, the speed-readers convert their minds over to reading mode and skip ahead to the end of the slide. So, by choosing to limit the amount of words to a few overview words, we are becoming more effective in our pitch. We limit the audience's tendency to be distracted by the reading and help them cue into what is being said by the educator (salesman/server/etc.) Again, we are wise to encourage note taking, so questions and answer sessions are more robust and effective.

Some do have ADD and will drift off during a sales conversation, no matter what tactics are employed. The best way to address these minds is sometimes through the question-and-answer sales pitch. We do need to engage the sense of this person in short sentences and with slow note-writing efforts, and learning does occur with nearly all people. If we notice the drift-off tendency in the person we are communicating with, it is likely time to do some reset.

"Could I trouble you for a glass of water?" This sentence often helps me pull back the person with wandering attention. First of all, it gives them an opportunity to stand up and get their blood pumping, and second, it gives them a chance to become the server for a moment. By switching roles or changing up the scenario ever-so-slightly, the audience is usually ready to re-engage.

The classroom setting, where one sits for fifty minutes to learn something, seems to be less effective than the "break-out session" way of conducting learning. Or when we take a bathroom break after the first twenty-five to thirty minutes, the next fifteen to twenty minutes after the break is more productive.

No matter how you choose to teach others, be tuned in to the human nature that comes with the person you intend to teach. We should be able to serve them, make them feel comfortable, and maybe even allow them to serve us. By accepting water when offered by the host of the sales discussion, we are allowing them to serve us and empathize with our plight. They likely realize that they would be slightly uncomfortable having to do what we do for a living and may even wonder how we are able to do it. But the more we become a typical person in the world, just like them, the more we are making good headway on getting our point across.

We all have needs and learn differently. How can you better understand your customers in the future? Remember to listen and be present at all moments. Notice all the small cues you see in the person you serve, and anticipate how to serve them better in the moment. The improvisational conversation is about to happen every time you give your sales pitch. If you see it as a canned "one-size-fits-all" sales pitch, you will be less effective. Play off the audience, figure out if they are slow-talkers or speed readers or maybe lack the attention span, and then use these cues to play the game the way they want to.

Service (& sales) is a great sport. We can make professional athletes money in this sport, and when we focus on the game, we forget we are even working. The people we play the game with make this possible.

Chapter 28

All Work and No Play

Makes Service and Sales both Easy and Hard

Where does mental instability come from, and why is it so hard for many people to leave their problems behind? In Jack Kerouac's 1962 Novel, *Big Sur,* the poet and novelist's setting is a cabin at Big Sur on the California coast. The setting is often a character in books and stories. The other characters come and go to and from various settings, but the story keeps progressing within the setting.

This reality, the concept of surrounding ourselves with a habitat that makes us feel better, is one to be assessed more carefully in one's capacity to give good service. If your setting is depressing you and makes it difficult to work, then is it possible to do work that changes your setting?

This is part of why sales have been appealing to me. Driving or walking past the same things every day, almost like the movie with Bill Murray, *Groundhog Day,* can wear us down. There is a big life out there, and so many variations on the theme of life are available for us to see. When we do work that helps us change the setting more often, the chances of feeling more exhilarating results from our day are increased.

Some days, I fly to another town and start seeing new scenery all along the way. I talk to new people while on the journey, which brings all of my talents from the past to the front and center of my existence that day. Maybe a person on the plane is taking the same course of study as one of my daughters. Or perhaps the person helping me with customer service behind the counter at the flight I missed is aching to get out of the mundane life she has chosen. At the same time, two hundred unhappy people wait to talk with her about their plight, their flight, and their desire to fight while making it suitable.

I relish every one of these moments as an opportunity. Technically, I am at work, on a journey to the new town, to educate other people about how to save hundreds of thousands of dollars over the coming years on their power bill. But also, I am in life, playing a part as a calm and confident character who works to bring some more joy to the day of every person with which I come into contact. This is the key to finding enjoyment in life.

Even if the setting is unable to change, the mindset is for sure able to change. For fifteen years of my life, I would work in the same setting. During this time, the phrase, "All work and no play makes Jack a dull boy," would float through my mind in the early years. I would be looking out from the waterfront restaurant at the lake from time to time, and my mindset would soften. I would realize how lucky I am to have a position in such a setting, where the view of passing boats and smiling people playing on the dock or eating an ice cream cone would be a regular occurrence. Then, all of these people would come into the restaurant so we could serve them. Our goal was always to look at the people, really see them, smile at them, talk to them, and thank them for the opportunity to serve them today. This mindset made the sense that we were working to fade away. We bathed ourselves and our clients in service, which in turn helped us cleanse our minds of people experiencing poverty, which is *my* mindset.

Poor me. If you find yourself feeling sorry for yourself or your situation, then there is still much work for you to do on your service journey. Why is it that I can have fun with all the people around me who also just missed the plane? Why are some of the people facing their day so intent on making the negative situation they perceive into everyone else's problem? Let's take a step back and realize how lucky we are, maybe by adopting *"the first world problems"* phrase into our vocabulary or simply by looking at those around us and giving them a smile and a nod. We are able to live ourselves out of our tendencies to make everything about ourselves.

Selflessness is practiced. Selfish is practiced. Which one do you practice more? How does one go about practicing selflessness? The more hours we practice having a positive mindset at work, the less we feel like we are working. Even the phrase, *all work and no play makes Jack a dull boy* is one to reframe in one's mind.

Let's say you make money by playing basketball. Having been on the team and in adult leagues, I can see how fulfilling being a professional basketball player might be. While I am playing hoops, my mind is unaware of the workout I am doing and instead consumed by the game I am playing. What a privilege it would be to be able to play a game for work. So, how do you create the same mindset? What I have learned is how to make the work I do a sport. The Michael Jordans of the sport are those who put in the 10,000 hours and decide to become great. The mindset of these people is what allows them to become extraordinary people.

What do you do for a living? How can you turn your mindset into one that sees the work you do as play? If you can't turn your service into a game that you love, then it is pretty likely that you need to turn your love into a game where you can serve love. This means one must be able to visualize loving the work that faces them each day.

When we wake up excited to attack the next day and have a good agenda filled out (schedule) that will keep us focused on the bigger picture of service to others, we are excited to do it. The builder who taught me how to build homes used to say, *"Every day, we are in a game, and lunch is halftime."* I was in my mid-thirties before hearing his mindset, but I wish I had heard it earlier. In my earlier years, I couldn't often decipher why there were days when I didn't feel like working. I would find myself exhausted by giving to others and wish I could give myself a break.

This is natural, and yes, we need to have quiet time off to let our minds process the larger picture of our lives. Interestingly, it seems the more we process in the quiet (not with screens and chaos), the more precise we become on our goals and agendas.

Today, I spoke with an old friend, the executive chef of the restaurant company, who taught me so much about service and the importance of giving to others. She was always so upbeat and poured herself into her creativity. Having been a student of Les Dames of d'Escoffier, the leadership organization composed of women who have not only achieved success in their professions but also contributed significantly to their communities, she has become one of the great contributors to my life. To become a general manager in this seafood restaurant company, we also had to have chef training. It is essential to be able to execute on every level in your chosen field. Julie Child was a member of the d'Escoffier group. This is all to say that by connecting with others who want to do more than oneself, the efforts pursued can have a more significant impact. This collaborative mindset to serve others and do something greater than ourselves is the way forward.

During our discussion, my friend assured me that if we were serving people, we would be on the right track. She also said that she remembered my positive mindset and upbeat persona. Though I'm not trying to toot my own horn here, it strikes me that the work we do in our lives has an effect on others that is sometimes immeasurable. Sometimes, it is not until the person is gone that we realize what a positive impact we can make on one another.

Reach out to someone from your past and ask if there is anything you can do for them. When you are feeling the 'poor me' mindset creep in, just call someone and ask how you can help them. Join a group, and come unglued. You are able to become more amazing than you already are. Your mindset is malleable and can change for the better every day. Thank you for everything, Sally. You are amazing. Let me know if you ever need anything.

All work, as long as your work is played, is a fantastic way to make sure we don't see our work as work. Jack Kerouak had substance abuse issues. What if he hadn't? What if so many people in the world, amazing people, could get off the junk? We can help each other do so.

We are playing with our friends when we work on a grander stage, with lofty ideas and products that can help others...and we have the power to achieve unparalleled results when we learn and execute this mindset together. I hope to be able to help others each day.

All play, even when working, makes Joseph a lovingly effective and happy boy (or girl, or them, etc.)

Chapter 29

———

Inviting A Friend Over To Play

Even a Kid Gets This Stuff...

When a kid gets to have a play date, much of the day seems better than the typical humdrum experience that fills home life for the child. Early on, it was a pretty rare experience for me to have friends over at the house. There were already six of us boys at the home in the 1970s, so the parents pretty much had their hands full. We spent our days doing chores after school, then eating dinner, doing homework, and going to bed. The routine had to be systematic in order to ensure things stayed under control at the house. Dad was out fixing horses, but Mom needed us to keep up the chores he had left us as her priority for our spare time.

But on Fridays, we could have a friend over. I had twin friends who came most often, so my experience was a little different than the brothers. The twins and I would find ways to have fun doing my chores. With animals of all sorts on the property, they thought it was fun. So, with this fresh mindset, the three of us would run around and make the chores a game. In Mary Poppins, the song, *A Spoonful of Sugar*, always rang true for me. "In every job that must be done, there is an element of fun...you find the fun, and snap, the job's a game...*Just a spoonful of sugar helps the medicine go down...*"

The song became an anthem in my mind in the first twelve years of my life. So much of my life was work that it wasn't long before work became my habit. Having fun with the work was the only way to ensure satisfaction with my life. Luckily, I really didn't know any better. There were no screens or social media apps to distract me. All I had was the lists and the time in front of me to complete them. Mom would have a table full of warm chocolate chip cookies for us on the Friday afternoon play dates. My friends loved it, and it was always something for me to look forward to. Later in life, the cookies became my signature dessert to share with others. There is always plenty of sugar, some flour, vanilla, a little extra salt, and pure butter to make the medicine go down.

As the later years of school happened, after the family divorce, I added TV into the mix for my fun. I would turn on shows while I did my homework. Sometimes, instead of shows, I would have music be my friend. But there always needed to be something accompanying my mind when I was going about the work. It wasn't long before I had learned how to focus in the middle of chaos. We all started to have many friends come over after school to play basketball and hang out. But the work at hand and my homework still would stay at the center of my focus.

Friends would often make fun of me for going into my room to do my homework while they were still playing at the house with my brothers, but for some reason, having the homework done made me feel more comfortable then I went to bed. It would have been easy to start getting distracted by all the other things that happened in a day, but putting the work first had become steeped in me as a young boy. It was what I knew to make me feel good, so it had become my comfort zone.

Is there a way, with all today's distractions, to re-create this environment in our homes today? It is what my wife and I have tried to do with our children. While a list of chores isn't how we have chosen to approach things, we instead have focused on being there to help with the homework whenever possible and create a home with a safe and loving environment. The social media restrictions we have kept in place have proven to be an essential part of the focus. Being involved in the activities of the kids has been very important. For eight years, I would help coach the kids in their basketball and volleyball practices. They now pour themselves into extracurricular activities like plays, summer jobs, crew, friend outings, and speech teams. But they all have remained four-point students.

We have been lucky to have great kids. The recipe today seems to be more of a balance between work, school, activities, and sleep, but we have found sleep to be the most important of these. Kids need quiet time alone. Adults need the same in order to thrive.

When we fill every moment with some article on our phones, social media apps, phone calls with friends, or shopping online, we are holding ourselves back from being able to have the rest and money to pursue the type of service experiences that allow us to grow.

The Flow – Many talk about a work-life balance. I see it as more of a flow. Life and our bodies are water in a life cycle, much like the cycle of water in science. The river is headed in a specific direction, always toward the future, the ocean. Nighttime is when our ocean of thoughts blends into a vast solution of being and then evaporates back into the atmosphere of our dreams. The dreams, which are the other third of our lives, are every bit as important to our being as our waking lives. How could we be as effective if we didn't allow this one-third of our lives the time to reach the solution, which is the ocean where we work out the recipe for our lives? Work and home life are much easier to balance when one loves the work and the home life both. By keeping a reverence for quiet time, exercise, introspection, and sleep in front of one's mind, one is able to maximize life and flourish in achieving a service mindset. Go with the flow. This is all part of chameleonatomy. The little creature in us that wants to blend in and be a part of the bigger picture is a powerful force.

We want to belong. We want to love and to be loved. We want to be cared about, and conversely, we want to care. It is when these elements, or our recipe, are too challenging to achieve that we start to experience unhappiness and depression. The power to turn it all around and start flowing toward the ocean again, rather than being stuck in a stagnant pond, is within each of us.

There is so much energy in a moving river. The key is to be moving. Be working and loving and giving and becoming. When we try to become more than we are today by working on our flow and ourselves, we are in the growth mindset, and we are satisfied.

I do believe that a child understands these concepts innately. Sometimes, as we grow older, we get stuck in a moment, and we can't get out of it. U2 laid it out perfectly in their song, *Stuck In a Moment You Can't Get Out Of.* Listen to the music, and imagine yourself getting unstuck. Imagine yourself able to write down a recipe for yourself to change the way you have been doing things and instead find different ingredients. Imagine yourself giving love to others in order to achieve more love. Imagine yourself being able to forgive others in order to be forgiven.

Imagination is the key. As kids, we pretend to have fun with our work, and then it actually happens. I'm pretty sure *Peter Pan* had things worked out reasonably well. If we keep our beginner's mind fresh and are always working toward finding positive change in our days, weeks, months, and years, we are assured of seeing the line of work that we can have fun with, and we will also find joy within ourselves. Our lives are gifted to us. It is up to each of us to see the spoonful of sugar that helps us be healthy and love the entire process.

Our work needs to be our play. By serving others, we are creating playdates with others, and it is fun. Our job is then fun. We learn a ton about each other and start to have empathy for the lives of others, which makes us better at what we do.

The life of a service mindset salesperson can be one of the most fulfilling lives available to us. If sales don't seem like it is your thing, then think again. Align yourself with an organization that needs great ambassadors, then spread the word by helping and serving others. This will either pay you in actual money (as many commissions-only jobs do), pay you in whole heart (as working with non-profit organizations does for many), or both. You choose. But find your thing and do it. Have a play date every day. Serve each other, serve the children, create the proper flow, and get some sleep.

Chapter 30

Be Where You Are Excited To Serve

Even if it wears you out...

You will be in an interview with someone where the goal is to sell yourself. Welcome to the art of selling a product.

You are a product. Your company is a product. If the company excites you and the product excites you, you are home free. But first, you must sell yourself. What is it about you that people should know in order to feel at home with the prospect of working with you? If you seem to be in it for the money, the buyer will sense it. If you seem to be there because you love to serve others, the buyer will sense it. If you are representing a sub-par product, the buyer will sense it. If you don't like your job and show no excitement about being there to serve those you are pitching, the buyer will sense it.

Now that you have decided that you are aligned with the product and the company, you are in the repeated position of needing to sell yourself.

Here are some examples of how to handle the beginning of a sales pitch:

- First off, I am hoping to let you know why I have chosen to be part of (x) product and (y) company. Then explain both and what you love about them. Let them know what you will be telling them and why people are choosing to buy this product at this time.
- Secondly, I'm hoping to tell you a little about myself and how I found (y) to be the best choice. The exact path you follow will be the path you are leading the buyer down.
- Third, and maybe most importantly, the reason why I wake up excited to do what I do every day is (z). This is where you explain what representing this product does for (a) you and (b) the customers you come into contact with every day.
- The feeling of being able to help people solve their problems with our product and the right company is both fulfilling and gives me great satisfaction every day. When I am working, it feels like it is fun, kind of like being a cruise director or financial advisor who guides the clients to a better future.
- What are you hoping to get answered today? I'm sure you've done some research on the product in the past.
- How long have you been thinking about buying (x)?
- What are some of the questions you have brought with you about the whole process of picking the right (x) and (y)?
- Do you have any friends and relatives who have bought (x), and do they have any advice or points to consider for you based on their experience?
- Let me tell you some critical points about (x). While discussing, incorporate questions, see below for examples:
- We see people looking into (x) because of the problems they are trying to solve. Does this seem like you?

- What have been the main obstacles you've found that have kept you from buying (x)?
- If you were to incorporate (x) into your life, have you calculated what it could mean to your overall financial future?
- What do you most worry about when thinking of purchasing (x)?
- I have developed a two-minute survey to measure whether or not it may be a good time for your family to consider making the jump to (x). This part helps both of you get on the same page.
- Having been given a chance to ask all your questions, and after hearing all my descriptions, what still may be holding you back from jumping at making it happen today?
- We hear every day that people need a bit more time, which is very common. You mentioned you have been thinking about this purchase for (#) months, so you have obviously put some deep thought into it. I have shown you how you will save money and have a better quality of life and how the product will help pay for itself in the coming years in many ways. You both have said that you're on the same page, and we have no more questions. How about we grab the diem by the carpet and do what you've already decided you've wanted to do?
- I will be here for you at every step and will be your point of contact as the years proceed.
- We agreed we have the best product to solve your problem. I have been married for 27 years and know how to be there for people in the long run. I will be the best choice, and our company will be the best. This is the best product, so let's forge forward and make this happen for you both.

- Revisit asking if there are any questions you haven't yet answered.
- If you still have reservations, tell them again what you told them. Recap everything if they still have reservations and revisit the last bullet point.
- If they say, "Let us think about it again," then remind them again how long they have been thinking about this. And then tell them that they have three days after signing if they have any more reasons to cancel.
- Then, remind them how remorseful people are when they decide to cancel and re-tell all the selling points again about why they chose to move forward. Over 80% of the time, the buyer moves forward.
- Cancellations do happen, but the process can be revisited at the time a cancellation is discussed. Many times, the knee-jerk cancellation can be reversed by reviewing all the points of the sale. People wouldn't have come this far if they hadn't wanted to move forward.
- Please don't give them reasons to have reservations, and always try to find all the reasons to have no reservations.
- The purchase of (x) product is an emotional decision. If your process is focused on eliciting good feelings from the buyer, reminding them of things in their lives that make them feel good, and your process is calm, smiling and helpful, you may make the sale this day. Tap into good feelings, massage the good feelings, and make a positive forward motion on every play.
- Just like in many sports, it is essential to play your game with intent.
- I have massive confidence that the meeting will go well.
- Show excitement for the day and the people you are playing with today. This is the playdate that you have

been excited to have, and the same is usually true of the buyer's mindset.

- Make them like you. Make them want to play with you again.
- Make them want to tell their friends about what a good time they had working (playing) with you, and recommend they think of other friends that you may be able to help.
- References from the buyers are a huge key to your success. Help them think of friends they would want to help learn about your product and company.
- They already like you, so you will get the sale and the referral.

It can be emotionally exhausting to stay focused on the buyer for more time than feels natural. But it would be best if you made it feel natural. If it is time for a break, ask for a break. Ask for a glass of water. Ask to go to the restroom. Let them know that you need to take some photos of the house if you are selling a remodel, solar, or security. Ask them specific questions about their surroundings. Be excited about what you see. Don't appear tired or worn out by the process the buyer may put you through. They are in charge of their domain. But you are in charge of the meeting and need to keep the forward motion moving. It is you who guides the positive emotional feelings. If things get awkward between a husband and a wife, don't get overly involved, but be light and disarming. Tell them that what they are experiencing is totally normal and make them under-stand this is a decision that people don't face every day. Tell them how you have seen several awkward moments and have seen the cartoon balloons above people's heads said out loud several times.

Sometimes, the client is ready to roll and has no reservations. Other times, it is like pulling teeth to get past their defenses.

Remember, you're a counselor, a doctor, a dentist, and a server all wrapped into one. Your job is to fill the voids they may have and seek to understand them.

Ultimately, your job is to close the sale for their sake and your sake. They need you to help them solve the problem, and you need them to help you make a living. But it is about them. You are in business to serve others.

Time is both your friend and your enemy. If the buyer needs more time, you will sense it, and you will give it to them. But it is vital to save them from themselves. Analysis paralysis is the most common reason the sale doesn't happen. Sometimes, the buyer needs a permission slip to say yes. It is OK to ask, "Can we just do this thing and push forward this decision that seems very confident is the right decision for you today. What do we gain by waiting?" Be prepared to give more examples of the risks of waiting. Interest, inflation, and rules will change. We know that deciding today puts the buyer in control today. Control is what most people desire. Things out of our control could make postponing the decision to be the wrong move. If we know what we know, and we already have shown that it all makes sense as of today, then there seems to be no reason to wait. Waiting is often the same as losing opportunity. Today is the best moment in most cases.

If there are genuine reasons to wait, then honestly tell the buyer they are better off to wait. But if there are genuine reasons that waiting is risky, then also say to the buyer this. Make the case for moving ahead. There can be many reasons to "act now..." and though it may be cliché to say these things if done in the right way, acting now can help people save themselves from themselves. Often, people are their own worst enemy to their successes. Show them why this is often true.

In the *Head Full of Dreams*, album by Coldplay, the *Up & Up* song helps us remember how to keep going up and not allow things to pull us down. *"We're gonna get it, get it together, I know, going to get it, get it together and flow, going to get it, get it together and go…"* In the Super Bowl 50 halftime show, I was fixated on this song and then bought the album. *"And you can say what it is, or gift for it, close your mind or take a risk…You can say it's mine and clench your fist, or see each sunrise as a gift…"* These words help me to see that they are all in my mind. The way to achieve what I want to achieve is to visualize what I would like to achieve and then devise a solution to realize what was visualized.

Play out things beforehand, rehearse being received with a favorable reception. How is this achieved? Through an upbeat delivery. Deliver positives, then receive positives. Deliver a smile, then receive a smile. Deliver information, then receive information. Imagine how you will act and how you will present yourself, then imagine how your response will be to your having been excited to see the client show them how you can help them solve their problems.

There is so much repetition in becoming great at sales. Much the same way that the doctor practices his trade (it is a practice, after all…), you will practice your trade. You will imagine getting paid like a doctor if you want to do so, then you will provide the type of service that ends up helping you achieve that end.

The best way to achieve repetition is to put yourself out there in front of clients repeatedly. Have a busy practice because you love what you do, are good at it, and are striving to be greater than you are today.

Chapter 31

Living in the Moment

While Planning for The Next

The greatest thing about working in the service (& sales) industry is the daily contact with people. Try working in a vacuum, without any contact with the outside world sometimes, and it quickly becomes apparent that we need one another.

As pack animals, we do love the time we spend being around each other. A young puppy may have fun rolling around with our two-year-old children. It's all fun and games. Then, quickly, the dog gets older and starts to establish itself as a dominant figure to the toddler. This is when dogs begin to learn biting as their technique for controlling others. The pack hierarchy is constantly in flux, even though dogs are domesticated. But we, too, as humans, have similar tendencies. This is part of why we get along with young babies naturally, but the teenage years tend to be more frustrating.

We wean ourselves off of reliance on others to establish our independence, but it isn't long before we realize we need the whole pack. We need community in order to thrive as a people and species.

A person in your neighborhood walks to their mailbox almost daily. How often do you say "hi" to them or ask them how the day is going? If the urge to talk with others doesn't come over you often, then possibly a service (& sales) position isn't the best fit for you.

Some people are good hunter-gatherers but are more growly in a one-on-one environment. The hunter-wolf that learns how to dress up like the sheep is an age-old tale, kind of like attracting flies with honey instead of using shit.

All these old phrases are designed to get us to realize that being nice to people at the moment will make it more possible to help them later. Some would say it is more feasible to sell to them later. However, that is the problem. These people are still seeing "selling" the person as their goal. Our goal is to help people. And when this also happens to help us, then that is even all the better. *"What large teeth you have, grandma,"* and the wolf responds to Miss Hood, *"All the better to eat you with..."* Even Little Red Riding Hood is a book about sales. He was persuading little Miss Hood to sacrifice herself for him. Not cool. What if there were a book about collaboration so both the girl and the wolf could eat and survive? Thus, *The Anatomy of Service (& Sales)* is a quick plug again. LOL.

The wolf may come up with some good ways to eat every day, but way back, he learned that if he were to befriend the sheep or the little girl and work beside them like thousands of years of wolves knew how to do, then the pack of wolves and the clan of cavemen could feed each other and coexist. This is actually how the first dogs started to become domesticated. Wolf and dog-type animals collaborated with the humans. Either the wolf killed prey, then the humans would take over the dead animal and feed scraps back to the wolves, or the caveman would kill prey and still feed scraps back to the wolves. Studies about this subject are fascinating to read if you ever get time. Coexisting was an adaptation technique for both species. And now our domesticated dog friends have their wolf pals to thank for their pampered lot in the world. We treat the dogs with more care than our children at times. In fact, in door-to-door sales, animals are a significant way to the hearts of humans. They are still feeding us, for heaven's sake.

Notice the moment you are in. Notice the dog or the cat and care about it. Notice the children because you, too, were once a child. Your mother loved it when other mothers or a grocery clerk or a shoe salesman said something nice to the kid and treated them like a human rather than a baby. Treat all the animals, plants, and humans you meet with great regard and reverence. Notice the mailman or the neighbor getting the mail. Notice the attendant taking the cash at the gas station (this line will date the book… about ten to twenty years from now; I am not sure this will be a thing.) Notice how there are others nearby all day long. Do you talk with them? Do you make them feel better about their day? Do you seek to understand them?

The world we travel through each day is a wonderland. This miraculous habitat, interdependent and persistent, is the most fantastic part of our lives and is often taken for granted throughout the day. We can collaborate to treat the world with the most profound regard. We will do so.

When we hear, *"Take time to smell the roses,"* we are being reminded to use our senses and appreciate all that we have. My mother lost her smell about a decade ago. Do you realize how lucky we are to be able to smell, or taste, or see, or hear? Many people don't have the luxury of being able to use all the senses. But somehow, like my blind dog and brother or my smell-free mother, they adapt and persevere and still somehow figure out how to enjoy the day and feel lucky to be alive.

Our collective resolve to endure our shortcomings and then find a new way forward is part and parcel of how we have become experts at *Adaptession.* Adapt, then progress. This is a synopsis of what it means to grow and serve. Adapt, then progress. Your sales will soar when you do so.

And for all the famous wolves and wolf authors in the world (Jordan, that includes you...), thank you for everything you have done in the quest to assess, improve, grow, and build upon the work of the other wolves. By working together, we can learn from our mistakes and be better on the next go-round. Life will be unique if all the wolves are nice to each other, and the world won't include biting and hostility any longer. If the dogs can get nicer over thousands of years, then, of course, the people can, too. Maybe a kid's book about the wolf that loved to serve is an excellent next step... World peace *may be possible.*

We must plan a world in which world peace is possible. How does the work you do today help to make this a reality? A book named *Choose Hope* about how to denuclearize our world does exist. It's a good start if we all read it. In order to achieve world peace, service (& sales) will play a massive role in the process. You're on your way toward helping...

Chapter 32

Vision & Strategy Drives Excellence

Know You, Then Know Them

K now you, then you are ready to know them. What does this sentence mean to you? When all the people who wrote the constitution got together to decide how best to create a country, this was a significant strategy session. There were undoubtedly things these forefathers (and mothers behind the scenes, I assume) didn't like about the past they had seen, and thus, they wanted to ensure whatever they created would be different and better. They also wanted to make sure it was a living document that had mechanisms to allow for change.

The vision to create a country is a mammoth undertaking. The strategy necessary to ensure any significant endeavor is going to work also takes a great deal of collaborative effort, hard work, and service (& sales) to one another. Leaders who embark on these journeys in an effort to affect change often share similar qualities.

- Honesty and integrity
- Confidence and big-picture vision
- Empathy and Humility

- Self-awareness and Authenticity
- Influence and Positivity
- Good Communication and Decision-Making Skills
- Accountability and Delegation Prowess
- Commitment and Passion
- Empowerment and Development of Others
- Problem-solving and Strategic Thinking Skills
- Respect and Gratitude for Others.

Most of the above were discussed in various chapters. This means that in order to excel at serving others, one must have many of the traits necessary to be a leader.

If any of these are missing, no matter which ones, it is not too late to re-tool and keep trying. No leader is perfect. No server (or salesperson) is ideal. Excellence is the goal, not perfection. But don't repeat the same mistakes; this is critical.

You are the leader of your own life. And if you learn to lead yourself well, you will be able to lead others toward a better way for themselves. When you sell, you are leading someone toward the water, and hopefully, you will find they are thirsty. My Dad, the veterinarian, would always talk about the "horse to water" phrase. He would fill in different words to make it sink in better. "You can lead a horse owner to common sense, but you can't make them have any..." Or maybe, "You can lead the money to the horse, but you can't make them care about it..."

It's always the big picture that is most difficult for people to see. For example, if we try to get people to care about the effect their choices have on the environment, it is a challenging point to get people to spend money on. But the more they do it, the better they feel about the effect they may be having on the environment. But if we lead the buyer down the road of choices and they can see how they are affecting their immediate budget, rather than some world ten years down the road, they bite on today's dollar. The buyer doesn't bite on future dollars. This is why only some people are invited into a room to help write a constitution. My mother-in-law bought solar simply because the wrong guy for her won the presidential election. Impulsive? Yes. She is typically frugal with her money, but emotion overtook her, and maybe a little spite.

We must help others see the vision and have a solid strategy for how their help can be pivotal to achieving the overall vision.

Here is a quick vision: I can see a time when people don't have to buy water, and instead, it spills saltless from the ocean for anyone to enjoy. I can see a time when the advances man has made with fire, and burning are a thing of the past, maybe passe. Thank you, Mr. Sun. I can see a time when power will be amplified, and we complete the dream of understanding how to create tiny amounts of power that multiply themselves tenfold or one hundredfold. Maybe by riding the Pelaton in the basement in the morning, we will make the power for the rest of the day. There will be a time when power is a human right, and great minds will have made the path toward this time. I can see a time when borders between countries are unnecessary because a peaceful world has achieved a complete understanding of how togetherness and community allow us all to reach our true potential. I can see a time when education, just like beauty, is in the eye of the beholder, where someone creates their path of learning, and it is OK to do so. I can see a time when no colors are defining our pasts, and there is no limit to the colors we dare to create. There is a time that will allow us full autonomy. There is a time that will ensure bullying ends. There is a time when our children and grandchildren will stand beside our graves and thank us for trying and for pushing forward without regard to those who aim to stifle better results and better times. There will be a time when fight or flight is no longer a thing for the human race. There will be a time when anything seems possible because brave people tried hard, and didn't give up, and had the belly for difficulty, regardless of adversity and the limitations of what had previously been possible. In the world, I can see anything is possible. The imaginations handed down to us through hundreds and thousands of generations of believers and dreamers who have come before us will have laid a foundation for what is possible. Still, we will invent new languages to describe things seemingly impossible to describe. We will break or bend the boundaries of physics, chemistry, and mathematical laws to find new rules and better laws that help us all endure past what we know. We can do anything, people. We will, together, do anything, people. Let's do this thing, people. We are the people, and we need each other in order to succeed through all the coming adversities we will face. But we can, and we will. And today, we shall start. It's *going time.*

Let's develop a strategy for achieving the vision together.

Chapter 33

I can't afford solar... Time value of money

You've got the power...

Not that I am fixated on the solar and green energy problem of our time, but every day, I am reminded of how difficult the challenge we face as a world. Today, I spoke to a group of realtors. These are all people who are well-versed in making a compelling argument for or against the purchase of a home. They are the experts who position themselves as the knowers of the market and the neighborhoods, all the pitfalls and benefits of homeownership, and especially how to get a deal done.

I was a little alarmed when I asked the group on Zoom, "How many of you that represent the buyer ask the seller to see the power bill before buying the home?" How many of you talk with the water company to learn the condition of the water and if there have been any significant failures in the city system or if any pending assessments are looming that will affect the rates? Again, I questioned them, "How many of you are aware that the gas bill for the heat will undergo a major overhaul by 2045 when it is illegal to burn gas in America as the source of heat for buildings?" It was quiet. How many of you would rather rent a home than buy a house? How many of you rent power instead of owning your power? The silence after my questions told me everything. A week hand or two raised halfway, about five seconds after the questions, but it was evident that my questions sunk in and were too hard to answer, even for the experts. People, we are failing each other in everyday business transactions.

It is our responsibility to take care of one another and inform one another of the complex realities we may face. We can't totally see the future and certainly can't see very far past the few years until another new election or another world conflict. But we can be better prepared. We can be more proactive. We need better leadership. We need to educate current leaders while we develop new ones. Regarding the realtors, RINO can't mean "realtor in name only..." but sometimes it does.

What happens if leaders (realtors lead the transaction), all leaders, don't seem to listen to us or appear to do what is in their own best self-interest? (Show them the money!) Things go sideways and stop working; this is what happens.

We are still able to vote, though. But when leaders start to question the validity of voting itself, then what? Isn't it possible that if we could focus on serving each other the truth, we would end up with more reliably truthful leaders? If we could focus on learning rather than being an echo chamber for sound bytes and old ideas, wouldn't that be better? *The missing link in the evolutionary food chain of leadership, sales, and so much of life is service itself.*

We have nothing to serve but service itself. It sounds better than talking about fear and fearing fear, though that, too, was a good message. It feels better, too. When the entire culture of information dissemination is turned upon its head, and entire news channels spend their political capital on backing politics or the capital, we have made a wrong turn.

Enter *Service News,* where all we do is serve the truth. Based on the sciences, math, reality, culture, and kindness, a service-oriented news service, where the negatives of the day are brought to our attention and solutions that research how to end the negatives, gets more air time than the problem itself. Much like the Service Awards from an earlier chapter, we need to lift the solution makers, the inventors, the doers, the "tryers", and the thinkers as the standard for which we strive. The positives of the day could be given more time than the negatives on *Service News.* The channel would highlight the fantastic teacher who has incorporated the parents to collaborate and volunteer their time by helping teach break-out groups about their expertise or profession, as well as other inspiring human interest stories like these on the channel.

It all has to start somewhere, and you might as well start with your ideas. If not you, then who (another kid's book idea…)?

When we peel back the layers of the service industry, we can see it is inextricably linked with our collective conscience. We want better for our children and our neighbors. So, what are we doing to help make that happen? We want to be cared for and loved. How far back have we peeled the service onion? It seems that service has taken a turn for the worse in nearly every industry. Time for a change? I just raised my hand.

Suppose we are casual armchair quarterbacks passively passing the buck of our lives to the next generation. In that case, we may as well admit we are either not curious or are, in fact, lazy and cannot see and change the future we are heading toward. When we talk about the problems, we pass around negativity and forget how vital positivity and solutions have been to the America we have built. Positives need the most air time; this is a fact for growth of all types.

Again, what are we doing to help make things better in our world and our country? What have you done today to make things better? What talents do you have to give to the world? What skills could you teach the youth of today? Internships seem to be a dying art, but they are necessary. The electricians have their apprentices and their journeymen. Who else is developing the hierarchy of learning within the ranks? If you could contribute anything right now to the future of the world, what would it be? And what are the small steps you are taking to start heading in the direction of your desired contribution? Do you have a position of power that could help others to grow and get more out of their own futures and human potential? Do you desire a position of power so you can be one of the people who change the future of service itself? What are you doing to develop those around you? This is critical. Absolutely critical. Teach someone. Let them grow. Take a chance on being a mentor, and give of yourself. Not later, but now.

People will disappoint you. This I can guarantee you. But don't give up on them if at all possible. Keep forging forward. Keep overcoming the adversity, and be a beacon for others who have yet to try the same path as you.

My word is that time is going by so fast, and it's almost impossible to believe I just started writing this book two months ago. I have been thinking about the book for decades. I have been working in the field of service and sales for five decades. A severe sickness that ended in brain surgery and a close brush with death got me thinking that time was escaping me. Then two more severe sicknesses, and another brain surgery topped things off. There is no end to advertisity. I am sorry I have waited so long to start pulling my thoughts together in a manner that may have a chance to start a more profound dialogue among us all. I am thankful for those who have taught me and for those who have been patient with me while

I learn how to do better with the talents and skills I have gained along the way.

I am by no means a person with any more significant potential than any other person. We all have our gifts. We need to learn how to use the gifts in ways that create positive change. Negative change is easy. Too many prominent figures have tried this route in order to rise to the ranks. Fear-mongering and othering those who may be a challenge to the power structure have been a tactic tried by many in the past. We all know it won't work. It will never work.

We love the country, even when it is growing and morphing into something that can be unrecognizable to those who live long enough to have memories from another era. If I had a choice to be born again, into today's America or anywhere else in the world, I would choose America, right here, right now, because we are on the precipice of becoming something much more beautiful than previously imaginable. Our country, and all the products and people it will and may produce, are born into a system of possibility and hope realized. America is a place where hope comes to learn how to grow up and how to be more enduring. It is a place where the fire of hope is stoked and tended to and revered by those who sit around it. America is a place where we "Get Hope Done!"

When people try to say that hopelessness is on the rise, I know in my heart it isn't true. People want to be part of the solution. People are more hopeful than hopeless by tenfold. They want more peace. People want to be more safe and want to trust one another. People are going out of their way more than ever to help one another. It's the leadership that is lost, not the people of our great country. We can lead the leadership and show them how our resolve for a more hopeful America is unyielding. It's not about being significant again. Instead, it's about serving the best of ourselves to each other. How could "being Great Again" even be a thing? Anything pointing to where we came from is part of backward thinking. We must point, and lead, forward. We must become better at being servers of people, and better as a people, and strive for excellence, and grow.

I want Grandma's cookies and farm-fresh vegetables. I want to help harvest the wheat we can serve it to ourselves and those less fortunate in the rest of the world. I want to give the power to make power back to the people. I want to thank the power companies for having forged a way to build a power grid throughout the country through the most inclement conditions and hard times. I want to know more than I knew before. I want to embrace the learning of others so I, too, can learn and then teach others. I want to hug all the teachers, doctors, and leaders who have poured their hearts into serving from the heart. I want to live in a world that allows every person to be unique and encourages people to think unique thoughts because when they do, we all win. I want time to be with my family and friends and want those with all the wealth to share their good fortune in order to create a more perfect tomorrow for those who lack the same resolve to find a way forward. I want to encourage people to find a way forward, and I want to help them do just that. I want to believe that chameleonatomy is possible throughout the world and may become a course of study for others to expand upon and pioneer. I want to be a synapse in the grand scheme of the world we know. I want to have a chance to right any wrongs I have left in my wake, and I want to learn from those wrongs in my search for doing right unto others and all posterity.

But it's not about what I want; instead, it is more about what you want. What do you want to be remembered for someday? How can I assist you in achieving your goals? Is there an idea or a notion that you have been pondering that may be the missing link to our collective quest for a more significant existence? Do you want love as much as you need love?

We cannot only make our power now, but the whole solar energy movement is a metaphor for giving us back the power that has been slowly being stripped from us. *SNAP! I've Got The Power!* If you haven't heard this one, go look the song up, and friggin' play it! Get fired up, people... It is time to move on with your life. Stand up and get moving. The lyrics aren't so much what this song is about. Instead, the idea of having the power when you're standing at the mic of your life and how this all makes you feel when you take control of your life is engorged with love for others and ready to serve.

I realize that most of us are renters where we live. But this concept of owning is a metaphor for your power. Take control of your financial future so you can help others. If you pay off your power bill or other bills, you can free up money for college for the kids or a yearly trip with family or friends. This is your money, and others are taking it and investing it and earning compounding interest on your money so that they can do all the fun stuff, and so they can keep control of the way things are. Things are... changing. Things are possible now. Earnings are just as possible for you as they are for some significant corporations, monopolies, or federal government. You can do the earning. You can curb your spending. You don't need things. You need people, and you need to serve yourself and others so we all have the power to do better.

Things can be in your control. Things cannot control you. If you buy too much, things will control you. If you serve plenty and make sure you are selling the right stuff to help others, then you are winning. Your art is fantastic. Your voice is incredible. Your attitude is contagious. Your creativity deserves an award, and you will find your awards in how you make others feel.

Be on the winning side of history, and for heaven's sake, be on the serving team. Make a deal with yourself rather than the devil. You, the person in control of your love, are now free to move about the country.

You've got the power. Can't afford it? You can't afford to have the power that you own. You need to own solar, or your car, or anything else that is worth not giving away your hard-earned efforts on as a positive first step. Don't let others say it is OK to live a life on credit. It is not alright. Wake up to this first, then invest in yourself second, and let's help each other sort out what is next for you. This stuff will pump you up when you start to live this way. Don't rent your life to others. Own it. You will change the world. You will change your world.

Chapter 34

Memories vs Perception

Share the positives, minimize the rest

Over twenty million people have signed in to watch Lera Borodisky's TED talk about how language shapes the way we think. Our language shapes our memories. Our perceptions are a reflection of our memories through a prism of feeling and remembered senses. What if we could speak more languages? Would we be more able to understand the big picture?

On a global level, there are words to keep us oriented in all languages. Many people in a group of distinguished people wouldn't know where they are in relation to north and south and typical directional words. A similar question, "Where are we now, and where is your home?" when asked by a five-year-old from a different cultures, would be an easy answer for them.

Every culture and language has different words to describe things or events. So what if we were to develop words to describe things more diversely? And in a more positive tone? As language becomes more homogenous, let's say, the American English-speaking mindset, it leaves us with a narrower view of how things are in the world. When we expand our horizons to work beside and travel with people from other cultures and languages, our mind grows. Our language becomes broader, and our view of the world becomes more accepting.

I traveled to Europe in 1987 as part of my quest to get a worldly education rather than an institutional college experience. I had decided that it was vital for me to see others in the world in their habitat and try to blend in with them. This was likely the early stages of my thoughts on chameleonatomy. By leaving behind my comfort zone and spending three months in over fifteen foreign countries, I have been able to grasp an appreciation for other people, their cultures, and their languages. I genuinely love diversity and people and desire a world that embraces all corners of the earth with a more cohesive strategy.

When I got back to America, I felt differently about my own country and started to really appreciate the melting pot effect of how our democracy was designed. The words in Lazarus' sonnet, "The New Colossus," - *Give me your tired, your poor, your huddled masses yearning to breathe free* - have more weight than ever in our country and for me. Having witnessed other countries being referred to with mean language by leaders in America goes against the loving mindset we nearly all share. But suppose you put the mean stuff in an echo chamber and have it played relentlessly until the pop culture machine starts to sample the negativity on its album of tired favorites. In that case, the stewing negativity becomes "a thing." Can we overcome this? Yes, with solutions and service to one another.

If a child were dying every day from neglect or policies that don't address the problem with good questions and solutions, and you knew some of the affected children, would you do something to help with the solution? Why are we more likely to help if we see the person? If a family needed help and you had the means or money to aid, would you, and do you already do so? If some of your tax funds could go toward helping to solve these problems without creating a lazy society, but instead find solutions that inspire daily service and work ethic, would you be more supportive of the government helping those less fortunate?

There are thousands of questions that can be asked about any problem. The real work is in finding solutions and then helping to put them into action. As we are the people who govern ourselves, we need a better collaborative mindset and need to ditch the political mindset. We need a different mechanism or working group that can more effectively tackle change with a diverse and peaceful mission. All of this is possible, and all of this will happen.

Every day, a person can help become part of the solution. Our country is set up to embrace the helpers and those that need help. For me, that is an everyday opportunity. I have been in both groups. When surfing the world of the elite, my attention to service suffered because with more money came more problems and more focus on money. I have learned well how to serve and now understand on a deeper level how to help people help themselves. So now, I will work to put these skills to use every day.

For quite a while, I felt as though helping people build a new or remodeled home and helping them develop their dreams was worthy of my time and energy. Yet, as I dug deeper into the larger picture, I realized I was helping more people who didn't really need the help. In most cases, they already had a place to live that was warm and provided shelter from the weather. These people wanted more. More things, more space, more luxury, more prestige, and more equity in their home, which is typically why the project was pursued. For those who actually needed more space, for instance, to take care of a special needs child or help grandma move into the family home rather than be in a nursing home, these were the projects I loved to help make happen.

But these are all primarily first-world-mindset problems. The same people could have just purchased a different home that fit their needs better without the building part. But I understood how the materialistic mindset breeds and grows, and I was guilty of sharing this mindset for a few decades.

When I traveled to Europe in my twenties, I had just enough money for three months, and I even had to ask for help for the last week from my mom. But that time in my life, with nothing, just living and traveling amongst others who had a life completely different than mine, was one of the fondest eras for me.

When are you most happy in your life? Take a few hours and try to write down one of the best times in your life. What was fulfilling about it? How could you revisit the mindset you had at that time to try to find a way to recreate a more fulfilling state of mind in today's world? You may have many negatives that still have to be solved if you're anything like me. But starting one step at a time, one day at a time, with a mindset, focused less on the past and more on the future is how to be there for yourself when you need yourself. We often hope others will be there for us when we need them, but what about being there for yourself? By being healthy, we are prepared. By thinking pleasant thoughts, we will emit pleasant thoughts. By wanting to help others, we will find our talents put to better use. By letting go of money as a means to serve ourselves, but instead, as a means to serve those in more need than us, we will have plenty. We will rest better knowing that others also have plenty.

Falling to sleep when all is not right with the world makes us tired. When we are exhausted, we don't sleep as well. When our mind is calm, we sleep well. If we have done our best to bring solutions to the day and for others, we are rested and ready for the next challenge. Just like the baby in Chapter One, having just nursed, and the mother, having just served, we can satiate our physical and mental needs through service to one another.

Being a cowboy as a child and raised in a cowboy and Indian world of play, I realize it feels better to get along and help each other out. And if we get bucked off, shake it off. Back on the horse, there's plenty of journey ahead.

Chapter 35

Every Customer Is A Library

A body of knowledge in us all

Wise men say only fools rush in, but I can't help falling in love with you...As a river flows, indeed to the sea, darling, so it goes, some things are meant to be...

Imagine what if Elvis hadn't been there to bring the song written by George Weiss, Hugo Peretti, and Luigi Creatore to life? All of these people were wise men. Each of them had their part in the overall piece of work, written for the Blue Hawaii movie released in 1961. All of these men were in sales. The same could be said for Dolly Parton or Arethra Franklin. Each had its brand and attributes and brought us to a place we hadn't yet been through music, service, and, ultimately, selling their songs to us.

Popular culture is an ocean of creation, and we are the rivers that keep flowing into this ocean. The flow is so vital to the growth of one another. Without this flow of creativity, our Adaptession to the world we were born in would have been slower. Technology has sped things up a great deal, which means we are learning more, faster than ever before.

The wisdom that starts to build up within each of us is like a dam of rainwater that has slowly risen over time. The body of work gets more prominent, so the water gets deeper. But we all came from the same ocean and are going back to the sea once again at some point.

The dam becomes a library of information that is stored for later, like a battery. We are lucky to have libraries and the thoughts and ideas of those wise people who have come before us. Unless we record our thoughts, our art, and our memories, ultimately keeping the flow of information kinetic, the dammed-up water becomes stagnant. Energy is created by the transfer of the dammed-up information from the libraries to and through the generators (us, the content creators), which then builds more energy for the coming raindrops of ideas that shall one day come from our posterity.

If we fail to trap the information that one person knows, and instead, the wise man dies, it is as if we witnessed the burning of a library. There is no way to restore the information gained from the world to the person if the person doesn't find a way to convey the information learned. The ashes of a library would be a sad event for anyone. Thus, when people close to us die, it is heartbreaking. There is no way to replace what the person meant to us.

Now, think about the fact that each person you come into contact with every day is a library in progress. They have shelves that house much different experiences than our own and are a place we can go and learn more about the world. Ask questions, and be one of the readers. When we read people, we are acknowledging how special they are. We show reverence for the life they have already experienced and are curious about how their past could better relate to our own lives or help us learn about ourselves and our community.

Who, if you could pick anyone, would you like to meet and spend time with? Are there people in the world that you look up to and feel you could learn from? Are there people you wish you could emulate? Here's a little secret...you can.

Somehow, my life has been blessed to have been around some pretty amazing people. Whether growing up with a Hollywood megastar, being friends with one of America's all-time greatest soccer players, working for a dynamic sales guru, meeting and helping a president get elected, or playing music with a world-famous drummer, there seems to be no end to what is possible in any person's life. But at some point, the library burns down. When it almost happened to me last year, I couldn't yet comprehend the repercussions it would have on how to live the rest of my life. But it has been sinking in as each day goes by. All of my days are a blessing and a gift. Could this happen to you? It will. I used to say, "If I die..." in a casual sort of way. Now, the "When I die" phrase packs a much bigger punch to my very existence.

What is unknown for us all is what tomorrow will bring. But we can know what we will get tomorrow if given the chance to get it. And we can know what we will try to Give tomorrow if we have a chance to Give it.

Try to see the future by making an inventory of your past. Find what is holding you back from exploding with a service mindset, remove those obstacles, and forge forward.

Read and learn all about the field you are in. Become a well-informed person with high curiosity and many interests. The more varied your life is, the better you will be at navigating the various situations and people you find yourself taking part in.

By putting ourselves out there and getting to know and understand the others we meet, our results will be infinitely more collaborative and deep.

Become, behold, behave, be alive - We need to pump ourselves up and have enthusiasm for taking part in the industry we choose. Eye contact, tonality, physical gestures and a smiling mindset demonstrate enthusiasm. Are you an actor? You are now. It's time to play the part of a person who serves others.

If you can feel that there is a twinkle in your eye when you're looking at someone else, you then understand what I mean. Try to see how the other person sees you, and then become a calming factor for them. *Become someone to behold and behave similarly to those you serve.* And above all, be alive.

If you are feeling down, it's time to get up. Again, at first, it may be as though you are in an acting job. So, if you are naturally depressed or struggle with self-confidence, start your service (& sales) career as an actor, acting the part. Eventually, you will no longer be acting. Trust me on this. The longer you act like you are excited about meeting new people and serving others, the more it starts to change you on a cellular level. Your mind controls your positivity. So act your way as far away from negativity as you can get yourself, and don't look back. You are unique, you will achieve measurable results, and you will set a new standard for yourself. Thus, you will have a powerful effect on everyone you know. This service mindset will catapult you over the highest obstacles and pull you through the most bottomless swamp. Your life is now changing.

Eventually, you are and will be *becoming* the person you work to be and desire to be. If you haven't yet heard the Rufus Du Sol song *Alive,* then get on it. Let go of your pain; let go of your excuses. At least we are alive. And the least we can do is help each other enjoy the life we share.

Remember, we are mostly water. We are part of this world and are part of the water life cycle. Your energy is stored inside us all. If you are in pain, it is possible to wash away the hurt and wake up new. Cleansing the mindset is a process; stick with it. Service (& sales) is a mindset onward.

One more song I love is Peter Gabriel, *Washing of the Water,* from the Secret World Live album. Crank this one to finish up the day... *"River, show me how to float..."* When you think things are too hard, you have the river to hold you up. Go with the flow...We are there for you. If you listen loud and closely, you can sense all those who came before you right there with you, cheering you on.

Chapter 36

Goals prevent Coals

Come in Hot, Show Them What You've Got!

This has been a rewarding exercise. You are running alongside me and those in your sphere of influence toward something different than what you had previously imagined for yourself. How could we ever have preconceived notions of the path our lives would go? It's borderline foolish to think we can know the obstacles we will face next. But if we have learned anything from this book, we know to be ready with the right mindset to attack the days we are served with grit, kindness, humor, and love in our hearts. And embrace the adversities you face, always.

The Anatomy of Service (& Sales) is a way of life. When I would mention to people that I was thinking of writing a book about sales, the feedback was always pretty mixed. Of course, it has been done before when someone writes a new take on sales, and then the concepts ripple out through the marketplace. But the ripples from throwing in one book don't have to stop at the shore. My ideas have been simple all along my journey. If serving one another were more about loving one another and creating a peaceful coexistence in this world we share, then we can get our own financial and national houses in order from the bottom up. One new person at a time, one new foundation at a time, one new idea at a time, one shared world at a time, one positive at a time, and one book at a time, we can and will get closer to the goal. The library of the future will be teaming up with books about adaptation, Chameleonatomy, and Equipoise. People will wonder why some companies have stuck the landing on increasing sales while others will be continuing their same old approach in a dog-eat-dog market.

Even dogs were domesticated from the wolves they once were. All wolves behold! There will be truth-telling in the service camp. We have learned your lessons on this for you; there is no need to test if it is true; it is. Service requires pure integrity. There is no reason to stretch the truth on the service mindset platform of sales. If our product needs work, we will tell you about it. If it doesn't fit your needs, we won't push it on you. If you aren't a good fit for our product, you will be the first to know, unless we know it first, then we will tell you. There is no room for pressure sales in the world of service (& sales) because money is simply a byproduct of our service machine. We use the byproduct wisely and make money with our money. Our money serves everyone, including our customers. We put our mouth where our money is (wait, that's dirty...), and we invest it in all stakeholders, including the customers, their families, and our own families. We trumpet the benefits of our product with people who love serving and love those they serve.

There is a new world coming in sales. We are selling to a new world (I took it too far on that one...). I wish people could step inside my mind for just a second and take a quick look around. It's chaotic in there, but it has to be in order to match the intensity of the job at hand. Life is short. My dad used to say that Joey's mind was a dangerous place to be. He could see the riding on the wall when I hung a picture of a cowboy at entire run on a horse next to my bed. Maybe that didn't happen, but things like this pop through my head every few minutes.

"We are in business to make money." How many times have you heard that one? The next obvious question is, "And then what?" So we make the money, but we skimp on service and start pissing people off? Or buy cheap product parts that have BPAs and are off-gassing from China and hope we can sell the company before the lawsuits come back to haunt us? Then we lay people off because it is "just business; don't take it personally...?" Everyone out there needs to remember that corporations are people running a business. The Wizard of Oz even had a person behind the curtain. And when you think of how that guy stammered with the puppy pulled back the curtain, you can imagine what I'm trying to describe what not to be like as a company. Don't hide behind the curtain, leaders. Instead, set a tone of honesty and take a little less profit while still being profitable. Greed is not good, no matter what you heard from Michael Douglas. Make it about service, not about the money. I could stand on this box of Tide for several tides, but remember, the rising tide of service will lift your boat.

Business doesn't need to be mean. It can be kind, caring, and loving. How many people say the world loves business? Everything seems to have become sterile and professionalized, maybe corporatized. The key is to find people willing to work with one another in a manner that makes all stakeholders excited to go to work. The collaborative environment, where results are synergistic, can extend past the corporation itself and to the families of the team members and clients as well. There is definitely a place for love in the workplace; don't sexualize it, people.

The goal is always the most challenging part. How do we set realistic goals yet still push ourselves? I'm a fan of being prolific and throwing a lot of spaghetti at the wall in order to see how much of it sticks. Here are a few final thoughts...

1. Set a goal to put service first in your life. Decide to be an authority and an ambassador of excellent service. Align yourself with a company that shares your mindset. Or make your own company, or be a 1099 contractor and go start hustling. The service bird gets the worm for its chicks back in the nest.

2. Make the goals you set for the sales you want to achieve easy to remember and measurable. For instance, I want to work forty weeks this year and intend to help four new families convert to solar each week. So 160 times this year, I will save a family (or the home, in case they sell to a new buyer) an average of $250,000. Thus, I will save American families $40,000,000 in the next 25 years from the work I do this year. And if I do this for the next fifteen years, I can make a $600,000,000 deposit into the pockets of everyday Americans. This will also give my family twelve weeks per year to be with me, which means over the next 15 years, I will spend 180 weeks with my family. The average job would be 2-3 weeks off per year, totaling up to 30 weeks. So, I can give my family six times more time with me by following this plan.

3. I intend to pay back past debts over the next ten years, then spend the subsequent money I make both saving for my family and giving 50% to programs that help lift people to achieve their full potential. Things take a back burner to experiences and giving.

4. I intend to keep health at the center of my plan. Ensuring I spend at least one hour per day exercising and 30 minutes per day stretching—well-balanced meals, with

  minimal dessert days (1 per week) on non-celebration weeks.

5. Writing and reading will consume at least one-fourth of every work week and 1/3 of every off week.

6. Sleeping will be calm and restful because my mind isn't cluttered with things or payments or worries. The truth sets our sleep free. A minimum of seven hours per night would be better, but nine would be better. This is when the dream gets put into action. Sleep is an equal partner to the wake, and when you've "woke," you realize all that talk may have been a dream, too.

7. Invest time into relationships. Both building new relationships and reinvigorating long-term relationships.

8. Find someone to help every day. Increase it to five people to help per day by five years from now.

9. Serve until death do us part, or until I lose too many body parts...

10. And...I want to become more remarkable today than I was yesterday through the Give and Let Give mindset.

There are so many different points to becoming comfortable in sales, but the most important ones have to do with putting yourself out there and being OK with some failures. In fact, be OK with a ton of failure. The rejections are what give us our superhero service mindset. Find the commonalities with those you are serving, and have fun with them. Bring joy to the lives of those you work with and those you serve. Be curious about your chosen field, and decide you want to be better at it every day. Find the points you are missing by asking others, "What am I missing here?" Ask others where they see room for improvement in your delivery and tone. Ask for advice on all sorts of matters pertaining to how you do your job. If you are too proud to ask, you will fall repeatedly.

Show those you serve how your diligence and tenacity will help them. Trumpet the reasons why you work with this organization and sell this product and why you are the best person to help them. Be sincere to be convincing. Smile twice as much as you think you should. Then smile again. Be situationally aware of everything, and use everything you see and have ever done in your sales process. Release endorphins in others by how you make them feel. Help them think about what makes them feel good. Their experience with you will make them feel good.

When you want the best for others, the best will be there for you, and you will be the best. I could probably keep rambling on this wrap-up for many more pages or books.

This is a process; we need to start at A and keep going until we have achieved Z. Adapt, progress (thus adaptession happens), and be a chameleon. Again, I'm here if you still have any questions that need addressing. Either my team or I will be in touch when you need help. Together, we can help you create the anatomy of service for you and your organization.

Now, as my twin friend Dave reminds me, I always used to say when we were kids when it came to work (which he has helped with many times in his life...). Let's *git 'er done.*

Circle of
Service

THE EQUATION
(Preparation +
Opportunity)
*
Adversity
=
LOVE
(success)

Self → God

others (neighbors)

Solutions

Future

World

Family

These "7" are critical:
Serve...

1) God   4) Others (neighbors)

2) Self   5) World

3) Family   6) Solutions

7) The World
(1 & 7 are bookends...)

Acknowledgments

Thank you to...

Katy, the girls, mom, Dr. B., the brothers, the sister, Kathy, John, Julie's , Jay, Anne, Cindy, Jordan, Jasons , Holly, Rita, Eileen, Christina, Renee, the nieces and nephews, Spines team, Frank, Sally, Budd & all, Andrew, Johns, Oscar, Coach, Chris, Matthew, Caleb, Russ & Jim, Will, Johnny, Ken, Morg, Farah, Nate, my infectious disease doctor team, my Neuro-surgeon team, my extended care team, the NIH team, the twins, Nancy & Janet, all the friends over the years, (you know who you are...) and all extended family, and all those million-plus people I have had an opportunity to serve over the years, and especially those so negatively impacted and affected by my poor past behavior. I will never forget the pain I caused... Service will bind us, money will divide us, Love will help us heal. The Anatomy of Service (& Sales) is a prayer for the world, we can heal.

I will die trying...

Love,

Joseph